A FIRST GLANCE AT ST. THOMAS AQUINAS

A FIRST GLANCE AT ST. THOMAS AQUINAS

A Handbook for Peeping Thomists

Ralph McInerny

UNIVERSITY OF NOTRE DAME PRESS

NOTRE DAME   LONDON

Manufactured in the United States of America

Library of Congress Cataloging-in-Publication Data

McInerny, Ralph M.
    A first glance at St. Thomas Aquinas : a handbook for
peeping Thomists / Ralph McInerny.
        p. cm.
    Includes bibliographical references.
    ISBN 0-268-00976-7 —ISBN 0-268-00975-9 (pbk.)
    1. Thomas, Aquinas, Saint, 1225?–1274.
2. Thomists. I. Title.
B765.T54M3923   1990
189′.4—dc20   89-40392

For Mortimer Adler

CONTENTS

Preface   ix

Resume of Tommaso de Aquino   xi

1. Getting into Philosophy   1

2. Philosophy vs Religion   9

3. Reviving Thomism   20

4. Two Big Pictures   32

5. Thomas's Big Picture   42

6. Theologian as Philosopher   57

7. What is a Thing?   66

8. Art and Nature   75

9. Causes   82

10. Parmenides' Problem   90

11. Motion   97

12. Creation   103

13. Soul   113

14. Beyond the Grave   123

15. Metaphor and Analogy   133

16. Proving God Exists   141

17. Speaking of God   148

18. The Meaning of Life   157

19. On Being Good 165
20. Aristotle and the Beatific Vision 172
Bibliographical Notes 181
Thomistic Chronology 191
The Writings of Thomas in English Translations 193

PREFACE

THIS LITTLE book provides a first, informal look into the vast world of St. Thomas Aquinas. I have tried to make it as intelligible as I could, using much the same style as I used in *Ethica Thomistica*, mingling argument with anecdote and example.

Thomism is solidly based on the assumption that we know the world first through our senses and then via concepts formed on the basis of our sense experience. Indeed, our knowledge of ourselves, of knowledge, of God, depends upon our conviction about the physical world. This contrasts in a dramatic way with a dominant alternative which, beginning with Descartes, starts with knowledge of the self and establishes the reality of the physical world. I am not here concerned to develop both Thomism and its alternative, but frequent references are made to what I call Modernity for purposes of contrast. Needless to say, these asides should not be taken to provide the best case for Modernity.

Many years ago an elderly Professor Joseph Bochenski said to a youthful me: "When you are young, you teach more than you know; with experience, you teach as much as you know; when you are old, you teach far less than you know." This book contains truth, but not the whole truth. Much of what is said, being said with great brevity, could be extended indefinitely. But that is what philosophy is, the endless pursuit of knowledge, the constant addressing of objections, the willingness always to go back to the beginning. This handbook stays very close to Square One.

Why write such a book?

A few years ago I spent a month speaking to some young

nuns of the Immaculate Heart of Mary of Wichita on our medieval heritage. I thought of them as The Woodchuck Lectures, not because they answered that old question, but because of the avenue the convent is on. In June of 1988, I gave a sketch of the Thomistic Revival at a summer institute at Notre Dame for non-philosophers. The following month, I taped thirteen lectures on Thomas Aquinas for Mother Angelica. In the fall of that year, I gave a course on The World of St. Thomas Aquinas at Cornell University, where I was the Rachel Rebeccah Kaneb Visiting Professor of Catholic Studies for the academic year 1988–89. All these efforts to connect somewhat difficult matters with their origins in common sense converged in this book, a book my colleague Jim Carberry has long urged me to write.

I dedicate the book to Mortimer Adler for two reasons, the first more important than the second. Mortimer Adler has devoted a long lifetime to making the wisdom of the West available outside the grooves of academe, addressing himself *urbi et orbi*. He has succeeded enormously. If I offer so modest a work as this in tribute to him, it is because I know he will approve of what I am trying to do in it. A lesser reason for the dedication is that Mortimer was the one to whom the epithet Peeping Thomist was first applied, by Time Magazine. Al Plantinga has several times in print given me credit for this phrase. Since I have enough to answer for already, I wanted to make the historical record clear. Of course Mortimer is not among the Peeping Thomists for whom this book is written. But you, presumably, are.

I want to thank the students who used earlier versions of this book. In particular I want to thank Brendan Kelly and Michael Paietta, my graduate assistants, for helping get this ready for the printer and/or performing various other tasks that not even Dante with all his ingenuity devised for those with sins to make up for.

RESUME OF TOMMASO DE AQUINO

Born: March 7, 1225
Place: Roccasecca, in the family castle
Father: Landulf de Aquino
Mother: Theodora de Aquino
Brothers: Aimo, Rinaldo, and Landolfo
Sisters: Marotta, Maria, Theodora, and Adelasia

EDUCATION

Primary education: Benedictine Abbey of Montecassino
Liberal Arts: Naples, Paris
Theology: Cologne, Paris

DEGREES

Bachelor, Faculty of Theology, University of Paris
Magister of Theology, University of Paris, 1256

TEACHING EXPERIENCE

Paris, Faculty of Theology, Regent Master, 1256–1259
Master theologian, Roman province, 1259–1265
Regent Master in Rome, 1265–1268
Regent Master, Paris, 1269–1272
Regent Master, Naples, 1271–1274

COURSES GIVEN

Commented on Bible, Old and New Testament
Commented on *Sentences* of Peter Lombard

Commented on Pseudo-Dionysius
Commented on Boethius

DISPUTES AND SERMONS

Disputed Questions
Quodlibetal Questions
Sermons on the Pater, Ave, and Credo
University Sermons

PUBLICATIONS

Collected Works, various editions
    cf. Appendix

HONORS

Canonized July 18, 1323
Revocation of 1277 Parisian Condemnation of his teaching,
    1325

1. GETTING INTO PHILOSOPHY

THOMAS AQUINAS was canonized on July 18, 1323 but he had already been put in Paradise by Dante who died in 1321.

Thomas's main role in the *Divine Comedy* is to praise St. Francis and his followers. St. Bonaventure, a Franciscan and contemporary of Thomas, is given the task of praising St. Dominic and the Dominican Order to which Thomas belonged. Dante saw these mendicant or begging friars as providing a needed reform of the Church. To this day it is impossible to think of Thomas Aquinas without thinking of the Church.

Councils and popes have praised him, saints and sinners have studied his writings, few philosophers are without an opinion of his main teachings. Somewhere, right now, there are people poring over his texts—over seven hundred years after his death.

Plato and Aristotle have been dead nearly three times as long and they too are still read. Moreover, there are Platonists and Aristotelians among us today. Whitehead said that we are born either Platonists or Aristotelians, presumably the way people in Gilbert & Sullivan are born either little conservatives or little liberals.

A lot of dead philosophers are still read but very few of them have followers. Thomas Aquinas is one of that handful. (He was born an Aristotelian, incidentally.) Of course it has not hurt his reputation that he is held in such honor by the Church and is the patron of Catholic schools. There are people alive today who remember whole batteries of college courses in philosophy and theology that were, or aspired to

be, Thomistic. Although that has changed, editions and translations and translations and studies of Thomas's writings continue to pour from
the presses. Journals and societies are devoted to his thought.
No one would want to read everything that has been written
about Thomas Aquinas. But then very few people have read
everything Thomas himself wrote.

Thomas has been recommended to Catholic philosophers
and theologians as their principal guide. The assumption is
that he can aid them in their task. Their task, in a nutshell,
is to attain the truth. The main reason to read Thomas is to
learn things that are true.

Platonists follow Plato because they think he leads them
to the truth.

Aristotelians follow Aristotle because they think he leads
them to the truth.

There are Platonists and there are Aristotelians, but there
are also Plato-scholars and Aristotle-scholars. A scholar is someone who knows a good deal more than you and I but it is
sometimes unclear why he wants to. Disputes over passages
in Plato have raged for centuries. The Platonist wishes to re-
solve the dispute in order to arrive at the true position. The
Plato-scholar resolves disputes, to the degree that he does, by
arguing that this or that is what Plato truly meant.

It could be argued that every Platonist must be in some
degree a Plato-scholar. If that is true, the Plato-scholar is a
truncated type. He is very serious about what the author actually said or meant. As to its truth or falsity, well, that is
another thing.

Sometimes Platonists get annoyed with Plato-scholars. St.
Augustine said that we do not send our children to school
to learn what the teacher says. What we want is for them
to learn the truth. Thomas said that the point of philosophy
is not to find out what so-and-so said.

Of course children have to know what the teacher says in
order to go on to what Augustine wanted for his son. Thomas
did not wish to deny that we must learn from those so-and-
so's who have written. Learn not only that they truly said

such-and-such, but also whether what they said is true—that is the point of studying them.

By and large, we think of truths as belonging to very restricted areas of inquiry. The more restricted the better. To know all that can be known about bees, for example. Which leaves out a lot of other bugs. And plants. And beasts. But you can't be busy about everything, so take bees.

Human knowledge is then the sum of all these special truths. And nobody knows them all. You might subscribe to *Scientific American* or *World Book* and read around in a lot of areas and in some sense know something about many things. Any scientist knows his field in that way. Bees he's an expert on, but he will take your word on mosquitos. In physics he's as much a tourist as you are.

One way of thinking about the many domains of knowledge is as an evolution from philosophy. For centuries the study of nature was carried on by philosophers. Newton still spoke of what he did as natural philosophy and until quite recently the holder of an advanced degree in physics was called a Doctor of Philosophy. Things have changed. It might seem that philosophy flourished before knowledge developed into the many disciplines we know today and now has been surpassed. There is some truth to that. Not much, but some.

We can see the limitations of this view by noticing the way in which scientists and mathematicians, heavy with achievements and honors, often turn to philosophical questions. Kurt Gödel wrote long letters to his mother on the subject of life after death. For every philosopher who thinks science has rendered obsolete the questions of philosophy, there are two scientists who turn from their discipline to consider philosophical questions.

Some Philosophical Questions

What is a philosophical question? Here is a list of some of them.

What does it all mean?
Why is there anything rather than nothing?
Is man mere matter or more besides?
Does something in us survive our death?
What is God like?
What makes an action good?
Is there an ultimate point of human existence?

And so on.

Like the man who was surprised to learn that he had been speaking prose all his life, you may be surprised to learn that you have often posed philosophical questions. Of course you have. It is difficult not to. Fascinating as the knowledge of bees may be, few would rank it higher than answers to such questions as we have just listed.

We read philosophers in order to arrive at true answers to those questions. Not all philosophers are helpful. Only a handful are. Most philosophers are pretty bad. You have to study them to know that, which is annoying, or you can take my word for it, which is dangerous and unwise. I may be one of the bad ones myself.

Getting Started

It will occur to you that you needn't run any such risk. If you have already asked some of the questions on my list, presumably without prompting from others, you should be able to come up with an answer to them as well. In some sense, you have already implicitly answered many of those questions and by reflecting on what goes through your mind when, say, you are wondering what the right thing to do is, you can develop a theory as to what makes actions good. This path is open to you; in one sense, it is the only path you can take.

Its alternative is to read or listen to what others have to say on the subject. But what they have to say will be somewhat like what you find you have already implicitly thought. You are going to have to accept or reject it. Alter or add to it. Judge it to be true or false.

If we couldn't learn anything on our own, we couldn't learn anything from others.

Still, there are advantages in reading and hearing others. They may have thought of things we haven't. We can cover more ground in this way. You or I could invent the wheel, but it is convenient that it has already been done.

There are people who know more than we do. Mechanics know more about engines, doctors about disease, insurance men about life expectancy, politicians about human gullibility. Just about anyone knows more about bees than I do. If I want to learn about such matters, I am well advised to listen to those who already know them.

A feature of philosophical questions, unlike questions about bees, internal combustion, and insurance rates, is that they are inescapable. They are important for everyone. Any human life is, in a sense, an answer to them.

If you are going to choose a philosopher to read you might be guided by the fact that only a few philosophers have followers today. There are Kantians, perhaps there are Hegelians, God knows there are Marxists if only in universities and in Central America. There are Platonists and Aristotelians. There are Thomists. The list could be added to but it would still be a short one. Your choice is thereby made easier. (I am assuming that you do not want to be a mere scholar.)

There is no way you can know, before making a choice, what choice is the best. The best choice will be that philosopher who helps you reach true answers to some or all the questions on our list, and others like them.

You could read *about* philosophers, flip through a history of philosophy and get information about what they taught. But historians of philosophy inevitably put a particular spin on their narratives—they may be Hegelians or Thomists or Marxists—so you will have made the other choice as well.

Still, this could lead up to the choice of a teacher. A master. A guide.

If your choice is not random, it is guided. You will be guided by the historian of philosophy, by a college catalog, by your mother or some other trusted adviser.

For reasons that will become clear, it makes a lot of difference where you begin.

The Catholic Advantage

A Roman Catholic who turns to Thomas, following the guidance of the Church, has a confidence unlike any other beginner in philosophy that he is off to a good start. Unless we throw darts or follow a whim—"I like leatherbound books" —we will be trusting someone's advice. The Church is a surer guide than anyone else.

It is well to get this right on the table now. The thought has grown up that religious faith is somehow opposed to or at any rate an obstacle to doing philosophy. I will be stressing the virtual necessity of the Church's patronage if philosophy is to survive.

Many secular philosophers nowadays have given up on reason, on our ability to know things as they are. They have also given up on our ability to know moral truths, certainly of an absolute sort.

The Church insists on the range and power of reason, in both the theoretical and moral orders. Far from threatening human reason, religious faith seems now to provide the only defense of it.

A TEXT OF THE MASTER

Teaching and Learning

Just as someone can be cured in two ways, either through the operation of nature alone or by nature aided by medicine, so there is a twofold way of acquiring knowledge, the first when natural reason arrives by itself at knowledge of things hitherto unknown, and this is called *discovery*, the other when natural reason is aided by someone else, and this is called *teaching*.

In things which come to be by nature and by art, art operates in the same way and by the same means as nature does. For just as nature restores health in one ailing of cold by means of heat, so too does the physician and that is why art is said to imitate nature. Something similar happens in the acquisition of knowledge, in that the teacher proceeds in the same way in leading another to knowledge of the unknown as one by discovering leads himself to knowledge of the unknown. Reason's way of proceeding to knowledge of the unknown by way of discovery is to apply common self-evident principles to determinate matters and proceed thence to particular conclusions and from those to others. Thus it is that one man is said to teach another when he proposes by way of signs the same course natural reason would follow of itself. The natural reason of the student, comes to knowledge of the unknown by using what is proposed to it as instruments. Therefore just as the physician is said to cause health in the patient by working with nature, so a man is said to cause knowledge in another by the operation of the latter's natural reason: this is teaching. So one man can be said to teach another and to be his master.

Thus Aristotle in the *Posterior Analytics* says that demonstration is a syllogism that causes knowledge. If however one

7

proposes to another what is not contained in self-evident first principles or is not shown to be included he does not cause knowledge in the other but perhaps opinion or faith, though even these are in a way caused by innate principles. For just as what follows necessarily from the principles ought to be held with certitude and what is contrary to them ought to be completely repudiated, other things can be accepted or not, given the principles. The light of reason whereby such principles are known to us is given us by God as a kind of likeness effected in us by uncreated truth. Therefore since all human teaching has what efficacy it has from the strength of this light, it is clear that it is God alone who chiefly and interiorly teaches, as nature interiorly chiefly heals. Nonetheless, teaching and healing in their proper senses mean what we have been discussing.

Disputed Question On Truth, Question 11, article 1 (in part)

2. PHILOSOPHY VS RELIGION

ONE OF the reasons it is thought, incorrectly, that there is enmity between philosophy and religious faith is that believers have answers to most of the questions listed earlier as typical philosophical questions.

The meaning of life? "God made me to know Him, to love Him, to serve Him in this world, and to be happy with Him forever in the next." The catechism answer goes through those questions like a bowling ball. And that, the secular philosopher suggests, is the problem.

The believer can't "do" philosophy because he does not come to those questions with an open mind. He already has answers to them so he cannot follow the argument wherever it goes. Worse, he holds his answers on some basis other than argument. He doesn't *know* these answers to be true, he *believes* them.

Behind this objection lies one of the more bizarre assumptions of much modern philosophy, an assumption we will discuss fully a little later because it enables us to put a finger on the radical difference between Thomism and many, perhaps most, other philosophies. For now, let us try to imagine the supposed condition of the philosophical neophyte who is not a religious believer. The suggestion of the objection is that he, unlike the believer, will not hold as true any answers to those questions he now finds are called philosophical.

The suggestion is that the mind of one beginning the study of philosophy is, ideally, a blank slate on which nothing is written. She may be eighteen years old, the eldest of five and a veteran of years of summer camp, but her mind is taken to be a bleak desert across which the winds of doctrine are for the very first time about to blow.

A caricature. There is no such person. No one seriously thinks there is. But many, perhaps most philosophers, feel that their first task in introducing Fifi LaRue to philosophy is to cleanse her mind and reduce it to the condition of a blank slate. How else can the philosopher create there from nothing the system that bears his name?

And of course, *that* assumes that whatever answers may be rattling around in Fifi's mind are, not to put too fine a point upon it, false. It is not necessarily assumed that, whatever philosophically warranted truths come to furnish Fifi's mind, they will be a wholly different set than that which was initially swept away.

The Universe of Fifi LaRue

The situation imagined, then, is something like this. Fifi has been taught to believe that the earth is flat. Her feet are, she walks upon the earth, she would bristle at arch comments on rotundity, her own or Mother Earth's. At eighteen, she boards a commuter airline and flies off to the big city whence she takes a bus to Upsilon U. Due to a computer error she lands in a course in astronomy where she learns that the earth is round. She is led to this truth by venerable Aristotelian arguments drawn from eclipses, let us say. She is never quite the same again. To place the balls of her feet on a round earth is to put the naive flatland of her youth forever behind her. The words do not come trippingly to her tongue at first, but she repeats them in the privacy of her own room until the shocking truth can be uttered aloud. The earth is round. That is to say, the earth is not flat.

There is, we can see, a relation between what she now holds to be true and what she hitherto held, a relation called contradiction. Not to be round is to be flat so that if the value of P is "The earth is round" its negation, $-P$, will be "The earth is not round" which is equivalent to "The earth is flat."

Why am I spinning my wheels? Because it may be said that Fifi, thanks to Astronomy I and the good offices of Aristotle, now lives in a *wholly* different world from the one she lived in before. It is often asserted that flatlanders and roundearthers live in radically different universes. It is important to recognize this for the hyperbole it is.

The earth that Fifi once thought was flat, she now knows to be round. If the two claims are not about the same thing, Fifi's change of mind would be like the change of scenery on a stage. The only common note would be her mind; there would be nothing on the one set that is on the other. But that has the unfortunate consequence of making the denial that the earth is flat tantamount to the relatively uninteresting assertion, "The earth that is round is not non-round."

But enough. What is my point? My point is that the religious believer is not alone in coming to the study of philosophy with a mind furnished with what he takes to be truths about the world and himself.

My second point is that there are some philosophers who assume that all such pre-philosophical furniture is false. It is that to which we shall return as MacArthur returned to the Philippines—with an eye to victory over our enemies. For now, let us look at different ways of holding truths.

We will alter our example and imagine that Fifi has been taught otherwise and that when she arrives at Upsilon she already holds that the earth is round. In Astronomy I, she becomes acquainted with Aristotelian and other arguments on behalf of the truth of that claim. She finds these proofs both sound and cogent. How now might we compare Fifi's second state with her first?

At first, we would note, Fifi would have said that the earth is round because she had been told it was. There was a globe in her fifth grade classroom; her parents told her stories of astronauts encircling the globe; she has seen photographs of earth taken from outer space. Her Aunt Betty told her the earth is round.

When Fifi was on the bus to Upsilon, a wicked man sat

beside her and undertook to undermine her beliefs. The earth is flat, he whispered huskily, but there is a conspiracy to make us believe it is round. Tales of astronauts are myths at best, stories planted by the CIA at worst. That photograph from space? He laughs a derisive laugh. An obvious fake. His voice becomes suggestive and syrupy. "The earth is flat as a pancake, my dear, and it is time we face up to it." Fifi arrives on campus a confused and shaken young woman.

How reassuring Astronomy I is against the background of that sordid episode on the bus. Fifi sits straighter in her chair, her eyes shine attentively, she sets down the proofs of the earth's rotundity with a care other girls reserve for new diets. In the days ahead she wishes she could encounter that dirty old flat-earther again and give him the response she was unable to give before.

Now we have the same proposition from first to last: "The earth is round." Fifi held this to be true before taking Astronomy I, she holds it to be true after taking Astronomy I. But more has happened than the passage of time. It is the *way* Fifi maintains that the earth is round now that contrasts with her earlier condition.

We could say that before she held it to be true as a matter of local lore. She had no grounds other than the anonymous say-so of her early environment. Everyone she knew who spoke on the subject stoutly maintained that the earth is round. Her Aunt Betty told her so. Let us call this *Condition One.*

Fifi, like every well–brought up child, has been to school. She has seen a globe. She saw that photograph of spaceship earth. On the bus, she might have brought forth these things to counter what the wicked man was whispering to her. Perhaps she did and he laughed them to scorn. A globe? A man-made object, a monument to ignorance. We have already suggested what he said about the photograph, so Fifi must have brought it up. This suggests that she not only holds the earth to be round, but that she has reasons other than people's say-so for holding it. Let us call this *Condition Two.*

Condition Three is had when Fifi maintains the earth is round *without fear of contradiction.* If contradicted by wicked male passengers on the interurban bus, she can counter with un-answerable reasons.

And now we can express the secular philosopher's objection somewhat more clearly. He objects that religious believers already have answers to some or even many—maybe, in principle, all—philosophical questions and these answers are held to be true on the basis of faith. On authority, that is. And this seems accurate enough.

What is not clear is why this is thought to be an obstacle to doing philosophy.

Is He, Popinjoy?

Imagine that Fifi LaRue is a Christian. A good girl, she knows her catechism backwards and forwards. Are there certain things one ought never to do? There are indeed. Moses was given the tablets of the law on Mount Sinai and Fifi, un-acquainted with wicked theologians, knows the Ten Commandments are as true today as they were the day they were given to Moses—and even before.

Is there life beyond death? Of course. Our earthly life is lived in the vestibule to eternity. It is a brief and testing period terminated by death when, blissful or damned, the human soul, rejoined by its body at the end of time, will exist forever and ever either in hell or in the company of God and his angels and saints.

Jason Popinjoy, Fifi's instructor, hearing this, has his worst fears realized. The girl is some kind of fundamentalist, as credulous as the pope. He manages not to manifest his shock.

"My dear," he says, "let me from this edifying barrage select one or two items. Among the things you seem to be saying is—so to put it—that the human soul is immortal and, if I understand you, that there is a mysterious entity called God."

Fifi's ponytail bounces fetchingly between her shoulder blades as she nods.

"God exists," Professor Popinjoy repeats patiently. "You hold this to be true because the Bible says so, right?"

"God has revealed Himself in the Bible and in Jesus," Fifi replies.

"Those are your authorities?"

He explains to her that she thinks it true to say that God exists because she has been told this is true. And of course she agrees. Why does Popinjoy think it pertinent to say this?

There are several paths along which Fifi might be led from her present condition. Let us say that *P* stands for "There is a God."

[1] Fifi believes *P* to be true.

What does 'believe' mean here? It means to hold the proposition on the basis of authority or say-so. [1] imagines Fifi in what we earlier called Condition One. But, if she understands Popinjoy, she might reply that anyone who reflects on the world, on the succession of seasons, the marvelous way in which butterflies come into being, the frisky frolicking of foals, the smile of a baby, a sunrise, on and on, will readily agree that there is a God who is responsible for all this.

That is a smile on Popinjoy's lightly bearded face. He now sees that Fifi is in Condition Two. She has, or thinks she has, reasons other than say-so or authority for holding that *P* is true. But Popinjoy is there to tell her that as good as no philosophers think there are sound proofs for the existence of God. If there were such proofs, we could have:

[2] Fifi knows *P* to be true.

What does 'know' mean here? If to believe is to hold something to be true on another's say-so, to know is to hold it to be true on the basis of other truths or because it is self-evident. Fifi reveals herself to be in Condition Two when she suggests that, since the world is an orderly place, there must be a cause of this order and that cause is God. Here the truth of "There is a God" depends upon other truths which are not held to be true on someone's say-so.

Popinjoy is suggesting to Fifi that the result of taking his fifty drachma course will be:

[3] Fifi knows P to be false.

This is the only Condition Three he can envisage. [2] could be expressive of Condition Three if there were a sound proof for the existence of God.

Whether [2] or [3] is the outcome of studying philosophy is a philosophical dispute. It is a dispute between philosophers, not between believers and philosophers. (Quite unsurprisingly, the believer, even if he is not a philosopher but is a Roman Catholic—will agree with the philosopher who thinks there are sound proofs of God's existence.)

Popinjoy is right to point out that most professional philosophers nowadays deny that there are sound proofs of God's existence. In most periods of the history of philosophy, however, the vast majority of philosophers held that there are sound proofs of God's existence. The student of philosophy will be struck by this peculiarity of our own times and wonder why so many earlier philosophers, most of them more eminent than Popinjoy, thought themselves in possession of sound proofs. Does Popinjoy know something they did not know? Surely this is a matter worthy of investigation. One hopes that Popinjoy himself will take note of this startling fact about our own day.

Beyond Belief

We have in imagination followed Fifi LaRue from Condition One and Two to Three in the matter of the roundness of the earth. We then suggested that a similar trajectory might be described by our young friend with respect to the existence of God or the immortality of the soul. But, of course, there are dissimilarities as well.

The faith on the basis of which Fifi holds that God exists

and that she herself will exist forever is religious faith, divine faith, a gratuitous gift from God.

The faith on the basis of which Fifi holds that the earth is round is human faith.

We are not surprised to hear that at Upsilon, in the matter of the roundness of the earth, Fifi will learn sound arguments on behalf of what she previously only believed or held on the basis of inchoative arguments.

Nor, alas, are we surprised to hear that at Upsilon—it is all too typical of its kind—Fifi will be told that there are no known sound arguments for the existence of God or the immortality of the soul. Popinjoy may even be so bold as to suggest that there are sound arguments for the non-existence of God and the mortality of the soul.

It may unfortunately be the case that pupils pour from Popinjoy's classroom convinced that we now know that God does not exist and that there is no life after this earthly one. Fifi LaRue, we are happy to see, is not among them.

Fifi continues to go to Mass and say her prayers and marvel at the universe while always acting with an eye to her eternal destiny. She rides the interurban bus without proximate peril to her soul. In class, she ponders her professor's passionate agnosticism with patience and compassion. Popinjoy is furious.

His fury is not explained by Fifi's intransigent refusal to accept the pellucid proofs he places before her. In the dark recesses of what he would not call his soul, Popinjoy knows that he does not know there is no God. He thinks there isn't one. He can cite reasons why he thinks so. But those reasons are never so tight that they convict his adversary, or even Fifi, of irrationality. It may even occur to him, though I doubt it, that we live in an aberrant bubble of time when it has strangely become a widespread belief among university philosophers that theism is untenable. There are some who would take such opposition as good news for theism—the same philosophers believe that the claim to know anything for sure is untenable. Once it was otherwise. Philosophers good and bad undertook the defense of religion, such philosophers as Leibniz and Descartes and Malebranche and Berkeley, even more dubious types as Kant and Hegel. Some of these defenses led others like Kierkegaard to want to rescue Christianity from the embrace of the philosophers. Of course we should not permit Popinjoy to stand for all the philosophers of the present time. He interests us largely because Fifi LaRue happened to take his course.

A TEXT OF THE MASTER

Knowing and Believing

The gifts of grace are added to nature in such a way that they do not destroy but rather perfect nature. Thus the light of faith which is infused in us by grace does not destroy the natural light of reason divinely given us. And although the natural light of the human mind is insufficient to manifest what is manifested through faith, nonetheless it is impossible that what has been divinely given us by faith should be contrary to what is given us by nature. One or the other would have to be false, but, since both come from God, God would then be the author of falsehood, which is impossible. Rather because there is some semblance of the perfect in the imperfect, the things known by natural reason are likenesses of the things given in faith.

Just as theology is founded on the light of faith, so philosophy is founded on the natural light of reason, which is why it is impossible that what philosophy teaches should be contrary to what is of faith, though it falls short of it. But they do contain similitudes of them as well as things which are preambles to them, as nature is the preamble of grace. If then anything in the teachings of philosophers is found to be contrary to faith, it is not so much philosophy as an abuse of philosophy due to defective reason. That is why errors of this kind can be refuted with the principles of philosophy by showing them to be wholly impossible or at least not necessary. For just as matters of faith cannot be demonstratively proved, so some things contrary to them cannot be demonstrated to be false, but can be shown not to be necessary.

Thus we can use philosophy three ways in theology. First, to demonstrate the preambles of faith, things faith requires to be known, such as what natural reason can prove of God, viz. that God exists, that there is only one God, and other like things proved of God from creatures in philosophy. Second, to make known what is of faith by way of similitudes, just as Augustine in *On the Trinity* uses many similitudes taken from philosophical teaching to manifest the trinity. Third, to counter what is said contrary to faith whether by showing them to be false or showing them not to be necessary.

Exposition of Boethius's On the Trinity, Question 2, article 3

3. REVIVING THOMISM

ON AUGUST 4, 1879, Pope Leo XIII wrote a letter to the world, an encyclical, which was named from its opening words *Aeterni Patris*. In English it was named *On Christian Philosophy*. In this letter, Leo urged Catholic theologians and philosophers to take their cue from St. Thomas Aquinas and he urged Catholic schools and colleges and universities and especially seminaries to give pride of place to the thought of Aquinas.

Thus it was that the Leonine Revival came about. Leo ordered a critical edition of the writings of Thomas, which all these years later is still in progress; courses of study, schools, journals, societies sprang up all over the world and studies of the thought of Thomas poured from the presses.

In the United States, the American Catholic Philosophical Association was founded as well as its journal *The New Scholasticism*. Other journals, *The Thomist* and *Modern Schoolman* were founded. As mentioned earlier, students in Catholic colleges and universities took from four to eight required courses in philosophy, courses based on the thought of Thomas Aquinas.

This sustained implementation of *Aeterni Patris* was helped by a series of reiterations of the role of St. Thomas in Catholic intellectual life which reached a culmination of sorts at Vatican II. Since then, every pope except John Paul I has repeated again and again the special status of the thought of St. Thomas.

Why? On the face of it, this seems an extraordinary thing. Imagine that there are 643 philosophers, say, and one day, strolling in the papal gardens, Leo XIII decides to pick one of them as the more or less official philosopher of the Church. We might feel sorry for the 642. Why were they overlooked and Thomas chosen? It isn't like a governor designating the begonia as the state flower, given all the things that happened as the result of the choice.

You might even wonder why the Church should care all that much about philosophy to elevate Thomas above all the others. Of course, Thomas was a theologian as well as a philosopher and the Church has a more than passing interest in theology, but even so, it can seem an arbitrary choice. Why Thomas?

The fast answer is: because what he teaches is true. Does this mean none of the other philosophers taught truths? It would be hard to fail entirely in the quest for truth. The reason is found in the fundamental characteristics of Thomas's outlook, and these are shared by many other philosophers, but Thomas had a way of writing and arguing that has survived better.

The motivation for what Leo XIII did has to be looked for in the way the Church sees the modern world. There may have been those in the nineteenth century who thought everything was hunky-dory, but the Church didn't think so. Nowadays it is hard to find anyone who thinks the times are fine, but there is little agreement on what went wrong. That things have gone wrong is something on which you can get a lot of agreement, and I mean among philosophers.

Leo in the nineteenth century was disturbed by things out of which our own troubles have largely come. The problems were philosophical before they were religious. Kierkegaard, writing earlier in the nineteenth century, said: The reason we have forgotten what it is to be a Christian is that we have forgotten what it is to be a man. In order to understand the Church's recommendation of St. Thomas as our chief guide in philosophy we have to understand the philosophical situation to which Thomism is the antidote.

The World Ill Lost

René Descartes (1596–1650) stands at the beginning. Rightly
called Father of Modern Philosophy, he effected a revolution
in the way we think about ourselves and the world, although
he himself was perhaps not aware how radically different his
approach to philosophy was.

Like many others, Descartes did well in college, learned
all kinds of things and then one day, in winter camp in a hot
room, put an unsettling question to himself. What do I *really*
know? All kinds of things clattered around in his head, of
course—he could remember this teacher and that at the Jesuit
college at La Fleche—but it seemed to him that he knew nothing with such certainty that he could not at least *imagine* it
was false.

So he invented a little game called Methodic Doubt. He
would sort through what he thought he knew and ask himself if it was not imaginable that it was false. The procedure
can be understood if we use some such schema as the following.

I think that _____.

The game consists of this: Is there any truth claim that can
fill in the blank which is such that I cannot even imagine it
to be false?

Obviously, Descartes does not propose to try to fill in the
blank with just any and every thought that occurs to him—
first, grass is green, then apples are red, squash is orange, sand-
paper is rough, fire is hot, water is wet, on and on and on.
He's got time, but not that much time. He has to cluster judgments into types in order to play the game.

The first cluster is made up of any judgment based upon
the senses. You can see that under this heading all the thoughts
mentioned in the preceding paragraph are included. Are these
judgments as a group such that Descartes can expect all or
some of them to be true beyond the possibility of doubt?

Our senses sometimes deceive us. You thought something
was flat and it's convex. The suit looked black in the muted

light of the store but outside you discover it is blue. The stick in water looks bent. And so on. You get the idea. We sometimes think something has this or that quality and are deceived in so thinking.

Now out of that commonplace observation, Descartes pulls a surprising rabbit. If my senses sometimes deceive me, I will set aside as possible candidates for indubitable truths any judgments based on the senses. His idea seems to have been that if the senses sometimes deceive me, the time they do so can always be now, and I cannot build my thinking on so wobbly a foundation.

Now among the things that are set aside by this move is Descartes' body. He can hold his hand in front of his face, bend over and see his toes, but he will not trust the testimony of his eyes because they have sometimes deceived him. For now then, everything grasped by the senses, including Descartes' body, is set aside.

Descartes' Demon

So what's left? In search of something he could not possibly doubt, Descartes has thrown out any and all judgments based on the senses. Is there nothing he can know for sure?

Descartes was a great mathematician and it may surprise you that he did not immediately fill in his blank with "2 + 2 = 4," which anything we cannot doubt is simple as.

$$I \text{ think that } 2 + 2 = 4.$$

Wouldn't Descartes be home free with that? Surely, he cannot imagine such a simple sum is false?

Oh yes he can. And in two ways. Remember when you did your arithmetic homework and you got all the answers, were sure they were correct, then were told they were all wrong? You couldn't believe it. You were sure the answers were correct. Your Dad was sure. And then the teacher had the gall to say you had to do the exercise over again. Which, under duress, you did. You got new answers, the right answers, you got a B – in math.

Even Descartes had that experience. Notice, he tells himself, that the feeling of certitude I had on the first occasion is indistinguishable from that I have on the second. I was sure I was right when I got the wrong answers; later I am sure I have the right answers. That being the case, I am unwise to trust that feeling of certainty. With that, all mathematical possibilities for filling in the blank go out the window that is no longer there.

As if he weren't too happy with that, Descartes offers another reason for doubting mathematical truths to be true. Imagine a malevolent demon whose task it is to whisper beneath our pillows at night that $2 + 2 = 4$. He is crafty, persistent, and smarter than we are, and so succeeds. The demon knows that really and truly $2 + 2 = 5$. The reason that sounds funny to us is that the demon has done his work so well.

A silly story. Descartes doesn't think so. Once you have thought of such a demon, how can you ever be sure he doesn't exist? This is not a proof of the existence of the malevolent demon of the kind Descartes will shortly give of God. It is the claim that we can never be certain that he doesn't exist. And that means we can never be sure we aren't being deceived about even the most elementary arithmetical claims. So long, $2 + 2 = 4$.

When Thinking Makes It So

Descartes has thought himself into a very lonely spot. He has lost the world and his body and now even the world of mathematics has become dubious. There isn't anything left but Descartes and all that is left of him is his mind. He has been reduced to a "thinking something." Moreover, something whose thinking may always be doubted; to think is to be deceived.

It is at this darkest moment of the game of Methodic Doubt that light breaks through. Pondering the possibility that "I who think may always be deceived," it occurs to Descartes that, even if he is always deceived about everything else, he cannot doubt that he who is deceived exists.

Even if nothing can fill in the blank of "I think that _____", which escapes the possibility that it is false, there is certainty lurking in the neighborhood. Fill in the blank with anything and let that anything be false. If I think it true, I am deceived. No matter, I cannot be deceived that I who am deceived exist. Descartes has from the nettle of doubt plucked the flower of certainty. "I think, therefore I am!"

God to the Rescue

Relieved to find that he cannot doubt his own existence as a thinking something, Descartes shuffles through his thoughts looking for any whose existence would seem to require some counterpart outside his mind as their cause.

Does the fact that he has the idea of apple and thinks apples are red justify the judgment that apples exist? No. In fact, Descartes finds no idea different from apple except one, and that is the idea of God.

Where did the idea of a most perfect, all powerful, and just being, creator of all else, come from? Descartes decides that he could not have invented it and, to make a long story short, concludes that the only possible cause of his idea of God must be God Himself. God exists.

What a relief! There are now two certified beings in the Cartesian universe, René and God. Things move swiftly now. Would God deceive Descartes? Of course not. This thought removes his earlier doubts, the world is restored, Descartes gets his body back and he moves his feet closer to the stove and wriggles his toes in contented gratitude. God's in His heaven, all's right with the world and with René Descartes.

Pope John Paul II on Thomism

The hundred years of the encyclical *Aeterni Patris* have not passed in vain, nor has that celebrated document of pontifical teaching gone out of date. The encyclical is based on a fundamental principle which lends it a profound inner organic unity: *it is the principle of harmony between the truths of reason and those of faith.* It is this that was uppermost in the heart of Leo XIII. This principle, always consequential and relevant, has made considerable progress in the last hundred years. Suffice it to consider the consistent Magisterium of the Church from Pope Leo XIII to Paul VI and what was completed in Vatican Council II, especially in the documents *Optatum totius* (On Priestly Formation), *Gravissimum educationis* (On Christian Education) and *Gaudium et Spes* (The Pastoral Constitution on the Church).

In light of Vatican Council II, we see, perhaps better than a century ago, the unity and continuity between authentic humanism and authentic Christianity, between reason and faith, thanks to the directives of *Aeterni Patris* of Leo XIII, who with this document, subtitled "On Restoring Christian Philosophy in Catholic Schools According to the Mind of St. Thomas," showed awareness that a crisis, a rupture, a conflict, or at least an obscuring of the relation between reason and faith had occurred.

Within the culture of the nineteenth century two extreme attitudes in fact can be singled out: rationalism (reason without faith) and fideism (faith without reason). Christian culture moves between these two extremes, swinging from one side to the other. Vatican Council I had already had its say on the matter. It was then time to mark out a new course in the internal studies of the Church. Leo XIII farsightedly prepared for this task, presenting again—in the sense of establishing—the perennial thought of the Church in the clear, deep methodology of the Angelic Doctor.

The dualism setting reason and faith in opposition, not at all modern, constituted a renewal of the medieval doctrine of the 'double truth,' which threatened from within "the intimate unity of the man-Christian" (Paul VI, *Light of the Church*, n. 12). It was the great scholastic doctors of the thirteenth century that put Christian culture on the right road again. As Paul VI stated, "In accomplishing the work signaling the culmination of medieval Christian thought, St. Thomas was not alone. Before and after him many other illustrious doctors worked toward the same goal: among whom St. Bonaventure and St. Albert the Great, Alexander of Hales and Duns Scotus are to be recalled. But without a doubt St. Thomas, as willed by divine Providence, reached the height of all 'scholastic' theology and philosophy, as it is usually called, and set the central pivot in the Church around which, at that time and since, Christian thought could be developed with sure progress."

It is for this that the Church has given preference to the method and doctrine of the Angelic Doctor. Quite other than exclusive preference, this deals with an exemplary preference that permitted Leo XIII to declare him to be "among the scholastic doctors, the chief and master of all" (*Aeterni Patris*, n. 17). And truly such is St. Thomas Aquinas, not only for the completeness, balance, depth, and clarity of his style, but still more for his keen sense of fidelity to the truth, which can also be called realism. *Fidelity to the voice of created things so as to construct the edifice of philosophy: fidelity to the voice of the Church so as to construct the edifice of theology.*

(From an address delivered September 13, 1980 to the Eighth International Thomistic Congress.)

Descartes' Own Synopsis of His Meditations

In the First Meditation I expound the grounds on which we may doubt in general of all things, and especially of mate-

rial objects, so long, at least, as we have no other foundations
for the sciences than those we have hitherto possessed. Now,
although the utility of a doubt so general may not be manifest at first sight, it is nevertheless of the greatest, since it de-
livers us from all prejudice, and affords the easiest pathway
by which the mind may withdraw itself from the senses; and,
finally, makes it impossible for us to doubt wherever we afterwards discover truth.

In the Second, the mind which, in the exercise of the freedom peculiar to itself, supposes that no object is, of the existence of which it has even the slightest doubt, finds that,
meanwhile, it must itself exist. And this point is likewise of
the highest moment, for the mind is thus enabled easily to
distinguish what pertains to itself, that is, to the intellectual
nature, from what is to be referred to the body. But since some,
perhaps, will expect, at this stage of our progress, a statement
of the reasons which establish the doctrine of the immortality
of the soul, I think it proper here to make such aware, that
it was my aim to write nothing of which I could not give
exact demonstration, and that I therefore felt myself obliged
to adopt an order similar to that in use among the geometers,
viz., to premise all upon which the proposition in question
depends, before coming to any conclusion respecting it. Now,
the first and chief prerequisite for the knowledge of the immortality of the soul is our being able to form the clearest
possible conception (*conceptus* — concept) of the soul itself, and
such as shall be absolutely distinct from all our notions of
body; and how this is to be accomplished is there shown. There
is required, besides this, the assurance that all objects which
we clearly and distinctly think are true (really exist) in that
very mode in which we think them: and this could not be
established previously to the Fourth Meditation. Farther, it
is necessary, for the same purpose, that we possess a distinct
conception of corporeal nature, which is given partly in the
Second and partly in the Fifth and Sixth Meditations. And,
finally, on these grounds, we are necessitated to conclude, that
all those objects which are clearly and distinctly conceived

to be diverse substances, as mind and body, are substances really reciprocally distinct; and this inference is made in the Sixth Meditation. The absolute distinction of mind and body is, besides, confirmed in this Second Meditation, by showing that we cannot conceive body unless as divisible; while, on the other hand, mind cannot be conceived unless as indivisible. For we are not able to conceive the half of a mind, as we can of any body, however small, so that the natures of these two substances are to be held, not only as diverse, but even in some measure as contraries. I have not, however, pursued this discussion further in the present treatise, as well for the reason that these considerations are sufficient to show that the destruction of the mind does not follow from the corruption of the body, and thus to afford to men the hope of a future life, as also because the premises from which it is competent for us to infer the immortality of the soul, involve an explication of the whole principles of physics: in order to establish, in the first place, that generally all substances, that is, all things which can exist only in consequence of having been created by God, are in their own nature incorruptible, and can never cease to be, unless God himself, by refusing his concurrence to them, reduce them to nothing; and, in the second place, that body, taken generally, is a substance, and therefore can never perish, but that the human body, in as far as it differs from other bodies, is constituted only by a certain configuration of members, and by other accidents of this sort, while the human mind is not made up of accidents, but is a pure substance. For although all the accidents of the mind be changed—although, for example, it think certain things, will others, and perceive others, the mind itself does not vary with these changes; while, on the contrary, the human body is no longer the same if a change take place in the form of any of its parts: from which it follows that the body may, indeed, without difficulty perish, but that the mind is in its own nature immortal.

In the Third Meditation, I have unfolded at sufficient length, as appears to me, my chief argument for the existence of God.

But yet, since I was there desirous to avoid the use of comparisons taken from material objects, that I might withdraw, as far as possible, the minds of my readers from the senses, numerous obscurities perhaps remain, which, however, will, I trust, be afterwards entirely removed in the replies to the objections: thus, among other things, it may be difficult to understand how the idea of a being absolutely perfect, which is found in our minds, possesses so much objective reality [i.e., participates by representation in so many degrees of being and perfection] that it must be held to arise from a course absolutely perfect. This is illustrated in the replies by the comparison of a highly perfect machine, the idea of which exists in the mind of some workmen; for as the objective (i.e., representative) perfection of this idea must have some cause, viz., either the science of the workman, or of some other person from whom he has received the idea, in the same way the idea of God, which is found in us, demands God himself for its cause.

In the Fourth, it is shown that all which we clearly and distinctly perceive (apprehend) is true; and, at the same time, is explained wherein consists the nature of error; points that require to be known as well for confirming the preceding truths, as for the better understanding of those that are to follow. But, meanwhile, it must be observed, that I do not at all there treat of Sin, that is, of error committed in the pursuit of good and evil, but of that sort alone which arises in the determination of the true and the false. Nor do I refer to matters of faith, or to the conduct of life, but only to what regards speculative truths, and such as are known by means of the natural light alone.

In the Fifth, besides the illustration of corporeal nature, taken generically, a new demonstration is given of the existence of God, not free, perhaps, any more than the former, from certain difficulties, but of these the solution will be found in the replies to the objections. I further show in what sense it is true that the certitude of geometrical demonstrations themselves is dependent on the knowledge of God.

Finally, in the Sixth, the act of the understanding (*intellectio*) is distinguished from that of the imagination (*imaginatio*); the marks of this distinction are described; the human mind is shown to be really distinct from the body, and, nevertheless, to be so closely conjoined therewith, as together to form, as it were, a unity. The whole of the errors which arise from the senses are brought under review, while the means of avoiding them are pointed out; and, finally, all the grounds are adduced from which the existence of material objects may be inferred; not, however, because I deemed them of great utility in establishing what they prove, viz. that there is in reality a world, that men are possessed of bodies, and the like, the truth of which no one of sound mind ever seriously doubted; but because, from a close consideration of them, it is perceived that they are neither so strong nor clear as the reasonings which conduct us to the knowledge of our mind and of God; so that the latter are, of all which come under human knowledge, the most certain and manifest—a conclusion which it was my single aim in these Meditations to establish; on which account I here omit mention of the various other questions which, in the course of the discussion, I had occasion likewise to consider.

Translation by John Veitch, 1853.

4. TWO BIG PICTURES

I HAVE gone on at this length about Descartes because he conveniently represents the alternative to St. Thomas Aquinas. Not only that, he started something that continued to develop along the lines he had set down and ended by being something I am going to call Modernity.

By this I shall mean the big picture or view of the world that is opposed to the big picture or view of the world we find in Thomas Aquinas. Moreover, Modernity as I use the term here is incompatible with the faith. That is why the Church has put the stamp of her approval on Thomas.

When Leo XIII singled out Thomas, he had in mind a lot more than one man. I think he had in mind a tradition which reached its culmination in Thomas Aquinas. I am going to call that tradition the Classical view. It would be more accurate to call it the Aristotelian outlook, but I will use Classical to designate it, just as I call the opposed picture Modern rather than Cartesian. Probably no two terms have been more abused than classical and modern so they are tough enough to survive my use of them.

Aspects of Modernity

The Cartesian method arrives at the claim that the self is prior to the world, that our certainty of our own existence is greater than our certainty that the world exists. Indeed, we arrive at certainty of the existence of God *and then* derive from features of God the reliability of knowledge of the world.

The knowing subject first knows himself and then infers the existence of the world, of anything other than himself.

32

The notion that we already and first know many things for sure about the world is regarded as naive and this has an important impact on what one takes philosophy to be and what learning it is like.

Philosophizing is said to begin with doubt. The philosophical life is pictured as casting a wary eye on ordinary claims to knowledge, cleansing our minds, making a blank slate of it, in search of a starting point of thinking.

The first defensible thinking we do takes place *after* we have begun the study of philosophy. Whatever thinking you do prior to that is by definition suspect and has to be subjected to doubt if not outright skepticism.

This approach is not confined to Descartes. In fact, it becomes a common thread, with more and more of the features of things we know said to derive from our knowing, and less and less to belong to the thing itself.

Kant put his mark on the movement by, in effect, saying that we only know things as we know them. That sounds reasonable enough. But he takes this to mean that we do not know them as they are. Things themselves are never grasped by us, but exist out of reach, in some way involved in knowledge but never really known. What we know is what we know of things, not the things themselves.

Kant obviously thinks that knowing things as they are would be the same as knowing them as we don't know them.

The things themselves have become idle, and eventually are dropped all together, when Hegel simply identifies to be and to be thought.

In Modernity, the world is measured by us, not the other way around. Man has become the measure. This is humanism gone mad. This is what the Church seeks to counter by recommending the study of St. Thomas.

The Classical View

Modernity sees itself as a concerted effort to replace the Classical view which it regards as outmoded. Descartes was well aware that what he was proposing differed from the philosophy he had been taught in school. The philosophy he had been taught in school was, in his estimation, a jumble of assertions whose claim on our belief had never been seriously questioned.

So what by contrast with Modernity is the Classical view?

Everybody knows for sure things about the world; things whose existence cannot be coherently doubted.

The things of the world are what we first know, and we become aware of ourselves insofar as we know the world.

Before we know the world, our mind is a power, a potentiality, a possibility. Knowing our knowing first is simply not an option for us, since knowing in the first place is knowing something other than ourselves.

This has an impact on what we take philosophy to be.

Philosophy is not the study in which we for the first time come to know things for sure.

Philosophy presupposes that we are already in possession of truths about the world and ourselves. Indeed, if this were not so, the teacher would have nothing to address. Teaching is an effort to take us from what we already know to what we do not yet know.

Human thinking is measured by the world. Man as maker is the measure of what he makes, but the world itself is not an artifact of ours. Our knowledge of it is true insofar as it matches the way the world is.

Every human being who is no longer a child knows many truths about the world and himself and knows them for sure. They are beyond doubt.

Moreover, every human being knows moral truths, knows at least generally how a person should act and what actions are never permissible. The moral philosopher can help us get clear about what we already know, but he does not *confer* our primary moral knowledge on us. Again, he presupposes that we have it.

These features of what I am calling the Classical view are enough to contrast it with what I am calling Modernity.

These big pictures are clearly different. They are opposed to one another. If you accept the one, you reject the other, and vice versa.

Which One Is True?

So what? Why not say that some people are comfortable with the one picture, and others with the other, and that's about it?

If you choose the one picture you will, of course, think it is the true one, but so will a person who picks the opposite one. That means that from the one viewpoint, the other will be regarded as false, and vice versa.

This may seem to underscore the arbitrariness of accepting the one picture or the other. Is the only way to appraise the one view to accept the other?

I want to suggest, first, that we are already recognizing at least one truth common to both views and, second, that this truth enables us to show that one of these views is unacceptable.

No matter which of these pictures you accept, you are rejecting the other. If Modernity is your cup of tea, you have dismissed the Classical view. If the Classical view is yours, you reject Modernity.

If this is so, it reveals a truth common to both sides. Both sides accept as beyond question the claim that to accept Modernity is to reject the Classical view and to accept the Classical view is to reject the Modern.

No surprise here, of course, since what is being accepted is the Principle of Contradiction, the rule of coherence.

$$-(P.-P)$$

The principle can be symbolized in that fashion. Let P stand for any truth claim, any proposition. The principle states that the proposition and its contradictory opposite cannot both be true.

$$P.v.-P$$

Either a proposition or its contradictory is true. That this is rock bottom is clear from the tone in which we sometimes say, "Look, either it is or it isn't."

When we reach the point of saying that, our backs are up against the wall. This is the final club in the bag. We use it when we want to reach beyond controversy to what anyone, even our opponent, will accept.

Little kids will chant back and forth, "It is," "It isn't," knowing it can't be both, no matter what it is.

If P is made to stand for Modernity, it will be agreed all around, by Modernist and Classicist alike, that $P.v. - P.$

Big deal? As it turns out, yes. If one of these views can be shown to violate intrinsically that principle, this will tell against it. I don't mean that any incoherence in either view discredits it. The incoherence has to be at the center, crucial, involved in a step without which none of the subsequent steps can be made.

Modernity is incoherent in this way. It has to rely on what it wants to reject in order to reject it.

What I have in mind is this. At the historical first step of the development of Modernity, in Descartes, the way in which doubt is cast on all judgments based on the senses is incoherent.

Descartes' senses sometimes deceive him. So do mine. From that fact, Descartes wants to conclude that he can never rely on the senses with the certainty he wants. That is, he can always doubt what they report.

Let us consider a standard case of being deceived by our senses. The stick looks crooked in water. This can cause deception only if it is contrasted with a case where deception is excluded. Obviously it is presumed to be a straight stick which appears to be bent when seen in water.

It is when the stick is removed that we say, Good grief, it's straight. Because we say that, we take back what we said earlier about the crookedness of it when submerged.

Even to describe this simple case of deception, we have to take one of those judgments as certain. Unless we do, there is no contrast, no deception.

If you want to make a name for yourself as a philosopher, you could insist that the stick is really bent in its natural habitat, water, and only when plunged into air does it appear straight. But your theory will have to take as regulative the stick in water in order to speak of our being deceived by sticks in the open air.

Let us now make P stand for "judgments made on the basis of the senses." In order to claim that we must dismiss all such judgments as at least dubitable, Descartes must violate the Principle of Coherence. He must employ $P.-P.$ He must trust his senses in order to doubt them, so he cannot universally doubt them.

That is why this small point is indeed a big deal. It stops Modernity before it can get going. Once it gets going, it proceeds with a kind of inevitability toward the loss of the world. The only world left is one "we" fashion in our heads. Man becomes the measure of all things, of what is that it is, of what is not that it is not. That was the claim both Plato and Aristotle showed to be nonsense. It is still nonsense. The Classical view, and preeminently Thomism, is its antidote.

That much more, a great deal more, can and should be said of all these things is, of course, true. In this book we are just taking a peek inside philosophy. This judgment of Modernity does not alter after further and deeper discussion, however. If anything, it becomes more emphatically devastating.

Why Thomas?

It is because Thomas is the flower of the Classical view that the Church has singled him out in the special way she has. Whatever Thomas has to say of the world, ourselves, and what we ought to do, he will begin with what we already know. He will assume we already know a good many things for sure. That this certain knowledge is often confused and general is hardly surprising. It is nonetheless certain and more than good enough to provide the presupposed beginning points of philosophy.

TEXT

Aristotle on the First Principle

There are some who, as we said, both themselves assert
that it is possible for the same thing to be and not to be, and
say that people can judge this to be the case. And among others many writers about nature use this language. But we have
now posited that it is impossible for anything at the same time
to be and not to be, and by this means have shown that this
is the most indisputable of all principles.—Some indeed demand that even this shall be demonstrated, but this they do
through want of education, for not to know of what things
one should demand demonstration, and of what one should
not, argues want of education. For it is impossible that there
should be demonstration of absolutely everything (there would
be an infinite regress, so that there would still be no demonstration); but if there are things of which one should not demand demonstration, these persons could not say what principle they maintain to be more self-evident than the present one.

We can, however, demonstrate negatively even that this view
is impossible, if our opponent will only say something; and
if he says nothing, it is absurd to seek to give an account of
our views to one who cannot give an account of anything,
insofar as he cannot do so. For such a man, as such, is from
the start no better than a vegetable. Now negative demonstration I distinguish from demonstration proper, because in
a demonstration one might be thought to be begging the question, but if another person is responsible for the assumption
we shall have negative proof, not demonstration. The starting
point for all such arguments is not the demand that our opponent shall say that something either is or is not (for this
one might perhaps take to be a begging of the question), but
that he shall say something which is *significant* both for him-

self, and for another; for this is necessary, if he really is to say anything. For, if he means nothing, such a man will not be capable of reasoning, either with himself or with another. But if any one grants this, demonstration will be possible; for we shall already have something definite. The person responsible for the proof, however, is not he who demonstrates but he who listens; for while disowning reason he listens to reason. And again he who admits this has admitted something is true apart from demonstrations, so that not everything will be 'so and not so.'

Let it be assumed then, as was said at the beginning, that the name has a meaning and has one meaning; it is impossible, then, that 'being a man' should mean precisely 'not being a man', if 'man' not only signifies something about one subject but also has one significance (for we do not identify 'having one significance' with 'signifying something about one subject' since on *that* assumption even 'musical' and 'white' and 'man' would have one significance, so that all things would have been one; for they would all have had the same significance).

And it will not be possible to be and not to be the same thing, except in virtue of an ambiguity, just as if one whom we call 'man', others were to call 'not-man'; but the point in question is not this, whether the same thing can at the same time be and not be a man in name, but whether it can in fact.—Now if 'man' and 'not-man' mean nothing different, obviously 'not being a man' will mean nothing different from 'being a man'; so that 'being a man' will be 'not being a man'; for they will be one. For being one means this—being related as 'raiment' and 'dress' are, if their definition is one. And if 'being a man' and 'being a not-man' are to be one, they must mean one thing. But it was shown earlier that they mean different things.—Therefore, if it is true to say of anything that it is a man, it must be a two-footed animal (for this is what 'man' meant); and if this is necessary, it is impossible that the same thing should not at that time be a two-footed animal;

for this is what 'being necessary' means—that it is impossible for the thing not to be. It is, then, impossible that it should be at the same time true to say the same thing is a man and is not a man.

Metaphysics, Book 4, chapter 4

5. THOMAS'S BIG PICTURE

THOMAS LIVED at a time when direct access to all the writings of Aristotle became possible for the first time in the West in perhaps seven hundred years or more. For those who read Latin but not Greek—Thomas Aquinas was one of them—this was the first time, period. Boethius, who died in 524, knew Greek and set out to translate all of Plato and Aristotle into Latin, but he succeeded in putting into Latin only a few of Aristotle's logical works.

However, translated first into Syriac and then into Arabic, Aristotle had a distinguished career in the Moslem world. In the twelfth century, notably in Spain where Islam and Christianity met, works of Aristotle hitherto unknown were turned into Latin. The trickle became a flow and thirteenth-century Paris saw the formation of the university, the quarrel between secular clergy and Franciscans and Dominicans, and, most fraught with significance for the intellectual life of the Church, the reaction to Aristotle.

The Quest for Wisdom

The term 'philosophy' for Aristotle is an umbrella under which all knowledge huddles. Whatever can be known, particularly insofar as it leads on to wisdom, is regarded as philosophical. Philosophy is the love of or quest for wisdom. What is wisdom? Such knowledge as men can achieve of the divine. Theology is the culmination of Aristotelian philosophy.

In the Aristotelian cosmos, the planets wheel round the earth, the whole being enclosed in a sphere of vast but finite extent. What lies beyond? Don't ask. Wonder at the night sky is the origin of philosophy, Aristotle says, along with marveling at eclipses and pondering the relation of the nine planets to one another and the earth.

On earth itself, there is a common stuff or matter which permits ordered change throughout the whole hierarchy of earthly things. Men and rocks have a common matter, but man is the epitome of changeable things. What sets him off is mind and thanks to mind this thing among things can come to know and thus to possess the whole order of things. Cosmos means order.

Peculiarly human doings, the kind of activities that set us off from everything else, involve mind. Sometimes mental activity aims only at its own perfection, that is, gaining the truth, but often knowledge is sought to perfect something other than the knower. Aristotle calls these, respectively, theoretical and practical knowing.

Practical knowing involves finding the means for the achievement of some end or good, and insofar as we can distinguish between that good which is the individual's, the good he shares with others in his household, and the good he shares with others in his city, Aristotle speaks of three practical sciences, ethics, economics, and politics.

Success in the practical order opens up the possibility of pursuing knowledge for its own sake. Thus celestial navigation leads to astronomy as surveying leads to geometry. Aristotle distinguishes natural philosophy from mathematics easily enough and then, with far more difficulty, argues for an ultimate science which he calls variously first philosophy, wisdom, and theology. This third theoretical science came to be called metaphysics.

Schematically, then, the division of philosophical labor looks like this:

Philosophy:
- Theoretical:
  - Metaphysics
  - Mathematics
  - Natural philosophy
- Practical:
  - Politics
  - Economics
  - Ethics

For two-thirds of these sciences there is at least one Aristotelian work that answers to them. Aristotle wrote a work in fourteen books called the *Metaphysics* and he wrote a *Politics*. He wrote three ethical treatises, the *Nicomachean Ethics*, the *Eudemian Ethics*, and the so-called *Magna Moralia*. We have no mathematical or economic works from him. It was in natural philosophy that he was most prolific, writing a *Physics*, *On the Heavens*, *On Generation and Corruption*, and *Meteorology*. In the sciences of life, he wrote *On the Soul*, *On the Generation of Animals*, *The Parts of Animals*, *On Sense and the Sensed Object*, *On Dreams*, and so on.

Pagan philosophy had been known largely by hearsay for centuries, snippets culled from the Fathers, some few books of Aristotelian logic, a partial translation of Plato's *Timaeus*. Suddenly, as it must have seemed, a vast library of erudition drops from the heavens. What to make of it was an understandably pressing matter.

The Errors of Aristotle

If the Fathers of the Church, many of whom knew pagan philosophy well, were of several minds as to its relation to Christianity, it is not surprising that thirteenth-century Christians were divided in their attitude toward this new learning. The matter was complicated for them because Islamic commentaries on Aristotle often accompanied the work itself into Latin, so that an appraisal of the interpretations of Averroes and Avicenna, to take the most notable examples, along with the text of Aristotle was part of the task facing medieval schoolmen.

It did not take long before disagreements between Aristotelian teachings and Christian beliefs began to be noticed. These "errors of Aristotle" motivated theologians like St. Bonaventure in their hostility to Aristotle. Masters in the Arts Faculty at Paris seemed oblivious to the theological difficulties and appeared to theologians to be adopting a schizophrenic view.

It is difficult to overstate how much hung in the balance in this controversy. St. Thomas the philosopher cannot be understood apart from this urgent need to figure out how a Christian should regard pagan philosophy in its formidable Aristotelian form.

Let us mention three of the "errors" theologians found in Aristotle.

The Denial of Personal Immortality—Aristotle sought grounds for asserting that the human soul survives death in the peculiar character of thinking, an activity radically different from a physical change involving matter. Guided by Averroes, some theologians took Aristotle to mean, not that your intellect and mine have this character which enables them to survive, but that some intellect apart from our souls, a kind of angel that thinks through us, survives, not you and me. But clearly this conflicts with the Christian belief that we are destined for an eternal life and will answer for how we have lived on earth.

The Eternity of the World—Aristotle held that the world and time have always existed; indeed, he denied that the world as a whole could come to be. But this seems flatly to contradict the belief in creation and creation in time.

The Denial of Providence—Aristotle describes God as thought thinking itself, adding that it would be demeaning if God's knowledge depended upon anything less than himself. This appears to mean that God does not know the world. And that conflicts with belief in divine providence.

Clearly these are central matters and we would not expect any Christian to be indifferent to them. What could he do but condemn Aristotle?

Coherent Christianity

In comparing the Modern and Classical big pictures, we mentioned the fundamental law of reality and thus of thinking, namely, the Principle of Contradiction. It is impossible for a thing to be and not to be at the same time and in the same respect. The reflection of this in knowledge is that it is impossible for a proposition and its contradictory opposite to be simultaneously true. The believer accepts as true that the world was created in time, that God's eye is on the sparrow and He knows the number of hairs on our head, that the human soul is destined for an eternal life. In all consistency, the believer must reject as false what contradicts these truths. It would be irrational for him to do otherwise.

On this there should be no disagreement among Christians. Thomas Aquinas would have no quarrel with Bonaventure in rejecting as false the above errors of Aristotle. Thomas differs from Bonaventure in two particulars. First, he is never content simply to say that whatever conflicts with revealed truth is, of course, false. Second, he undertook a close and painstaking reading of the works of Aristotle which resulted in a set of commentaries on Aristotle which have no rival.

The first step, again, is this. Let P stand for "God knows things other than Himself—indeed, He knows whatever is or can be." The Christian believes this to be true. By that very fact, he must reject $-P$ as false. And $-P$ is taught by Aristotle.

That might be the end of the matter, if one overlooked the fact that Aristotle did not simply assert that God is thought thinking itself. The claim occurs in reasoned discourse. If $-P$ is arrived at by way of discourse, reasoning, argument, that discourse, reasoning, argument must be defective if P is true, as the believer firmly holds it to be. The second step, accordingly, must be to show what is wrong with the argument.

Taking that second step carries one swiftly beyond hearsay, received opinion as to what Aristotle teaches. The second step requires a careful reading of the text of Aristotle.

This is the step Thomas took, and with surprising results. That he as a theologian would be interested in Aristotle follows from the historical situation we are indicating. But that he should have undertaken the book by book, chapter by chapter, line by line, commenting on Aristotle is remarkable because these commentaries with perhaps one exception are not the product of courses he gave. This was a moonlighting effort, and one undertaken, as our chronology makes clear, when Thomas was not short of things to do.

Translators of Aristotle, like Barker who translated the *Politics*, tell us how previous sweeping theories often evaporate before this sustained immersion in the text. So it was that Thomas's careful reading of Aristotle led him to a quite different view of those "errors" than was common among theologians. In 1270, four years before his death, and in 1277, three years after it, there were condemnations of certain propositions and in the case of the 219 propositions condemned in 1277, some held by Thomas were included.

In a nutshell, Thomas taught that Aristotle's description of God as thought thinking itself does not involve a denial of providence, that Averroes's interpretation of intellect is incorrect and that Aristotle is teaching personal immortality, and finally that while Aristotle did indeed teach that the world had always been he did not thereby deny that it was created; God could have created the world from all eternity.

Thomistic Philosophy

Thomas was not alone in calling Aristotle *the* Philosopher. Dante called Aristotle the master of those who know. As a philosopher, Thomas is fundamentally an Aristotelian and the schema given earlier is the one he often sets forth when providing a map of the philosophical terrain. Principal sources of Thomas's philosophical views are the commentaries he wrote on Aristotle.

But if Thomas is fundamentally an Aristotelian, he has an Aristotelian appetite for whatever he can lay his hands on. Thus, Thomas finds room in his philosophy for the Neoplatonism available to him, particularly the writings of Pseudo-Dionysius the Areopagite—pseudo, because he seems to have lived around 500 A.D. and can scarcely be the Dionysius converted by St. Paul. Thomas is hospitable to notions like participation that Aristotle dismissed as mere metaphor. Thomas is often said to have made a synthesis of all available philosophical currents, and this is true, but a synthesis is not a hodgepodge. The condition for entry into the Thomistic synthesis is compatibility with its Aristotelian base.

TEXT OF THE MASTER

On the Eternity of the World against Murmurers

If we suppose, in accordance with the Catholic faith and contrary to what some philosophers mistakenly thought, that the world has not existed eternally and its duration had a beginning, as Holy Scripture which cannot deceive attests, a doubt arises whether it could always have been.

In order to get to the truth of this matter we should first set down wherein we agree and wherein we disagree with our opponents.

Were it to be supposed that the world could always have been independently of God, as if something apart from Him could be eternal and unmade by Him, this would be an abominable error, not only in the eyes of faith but even among philosophers who maintain and prove that whatever in any way exists must be caused by Him who fully and most truly has existence. However, we must ask if it could be maintained that something always existed yet was caused by God with respect to all that it is.

Were this to be judged impossible this would either be because God could not make something that always was or that it could not come to be even if God could make it. All would agree on the first point, namely, that given His infinite power God can make something that always was. But it remains to be seen whether something that always was could come to be.

The claim that it could not come to be can be understood in two ways, that is, as being true for one of two reasons: either because of the absence of a passive potency or because it is conceptually incoherent.

In this first way, it could be said that before an Angel was made the Angel could not come to be, because no passive potency preceded its existence, since it is not made from some underlying matter. Nonetheless, God was able to make the Angel and was able to bring it about that the Angel came to be, because He did and it is. So understood, it must be simply granted according to the faith that something caused by God could not always be, if to hold this is to maintain that a passive potency always existed, which is heretical. But it does not follow from that that God cannot bring it about that some being should always be.

In the second understanding something is said not to have happened because it involves conceptual incoherence, on the order of an affirmation and its negation not being able to be simultaneously true, though some say that God could bring that about. Others say He cannot because it is a nullity. It is, of course, clear that He couldn't effect this because if He could He couldn't. Should someone hold that God can do this, the view may not be heretical but it is in my opinion false, in the way that the claim that the past was not involves a contradiction. Thus Augustine, in the book refuting Faustus, writes, "Whoever says, 'If God is omnipotent he can make the things that were such that they were not,' does not see that he is in effect saying, 'If he is omnipotent he can make what is true, as true, be false.'" Nonetheless there have been those who with great piety said that God can make the past not to have been past and it was not judged heretical.

Is there then conceptual incoherence, an incompatibility, between something's being caused by God and yet always having been? However this comes out, it is not heretical to say that something caused by God has always been. I nonetheless hold that, if there is incoherence (self-contradiction) in the claim, it is false. If there is no incoherence, not only is it not false, it could not be otherwise and to say so is erroneous. Since it pertains to God's omnipotence to exceed all understanding and power, one who said that something that could come about in creatures cannot be brought about by God would derogate from God's omnipotence. (Sins are not a counterexample, since as such they are nullities.)

The whole question then comes down to this: whether or

not to be created by God in its complete substance is incompatible with not having a beginning of its duration.

That they are not can be shown in this way. There could be only two reasons for their incompatibility, whether the one or the other, or the two together: either because the efficient cause must precede its effect in duration, or because non-existence must precede existence in duration, which is why it is said to be created by God from nothing (*ex nihilo*).

The first thing to show is that it is not necessary that the efficient cause, namely God, precede His effect in duration, should He so will.

The first, then. No cause which produces its effect immediately (*subito*) need precede its effect in duration. But God produces His effect, not through motion, but immediately. Therefore, it is not necessary that He precede his effect in duration.

The first premise is inductively evident from all immediate (*subitis*) changes, such as illumination and the like. Nonetheless, it can be proved as follows.

In any instant in which a thing exists, the principle of its action can be posited, as is clear in all generable things since in that instant in which fire begins to be, heating begins. But in sudden operation, its beginning and end are at the same time, indeed are the same, as is the case with all indivisibles. Therefore in any instant in which an agent producing its effect *subito* is given, the term of its action can also be posited. But the term of its action is at the same time as the things having been made. Therefore, it is not incoherent to posit a cause producing its effect suddenly (*subito*) and not preceding it in duration.

It would be incoherent to say this of causes which produce their effects through motion, since the beginning of motion precedes its end. Because we are accustomed to makings which involve motion they do not easily grasp the claim that an efficient cause does not precede its effect in duration. So it is that many unlearned men, taking into account only a few things, arrive at easy answers.

The fact that God is a voluntary cause presents no difficulty to this, because it is not necessary that the will precede its effect in duration, nor the voluntary, unless it acts through deliberation, something we would not attribute to God.

Furthermore, the cause producing the whole substance of the thing is no more restricted than the cause producing the form in the production of the form, indeed less so, because it does not produce by educing from the potency of matter, as the one producing form does. But an agent which produces form alone can so act that its effect is whenever it is, as is the case with the sun's shining. Much more then can God, who produces the complete substance of the thing, bring it about that His effect is whenever He is.

Furthermore, if there should be a cause whose effect does not precede from it in any instant in which the cause exists, this can only be because the cause lacks something: a complete cause and its effect exist simultaneously. But God lacks nothing. Therefore His effect can always be when He is, so He need not precede it in duration.

Furthermore, the will of the one willing does not diminish its power and this is especially true of God. But everyone who considers the arguments Aristotle fashioned to prove that something was always from God because a thing always produces its like have objected that this would obtain only if God did not act voluntarily. But even given that He acts through His will, it nonetheless follows that He can bring it about that a thing caused by Him should always be.

It is clear then that it is not incoherent to say that an efficient cause does not precede its effect in duration because God could not have brought about the self-contradictory.

It remains to be seen whether it is repugnant to intellect that something is said to be made from nothing (*ex nihilo*) because non-existence must precede existence in duration.

That it is not repugnant is shown by the remark of Anselm in the *Monologion*, Chapter 8, where he is discussing how the creature is said to be made from nothing. He writes, "The third interpretation of what is meant by saying something is made from nothing is when we understand it to be made and there is nothing from which it was made. Something similar in meaning seems involved when a man grows sad without cause and it is said that nothing saddens him. On this understanding, remembering what was said above, apart from the highest essence all the things that are from Him, are made from nothing, that is, not from something else. There is nothing absurd in that." On this exposition what is made is not ordered to nothing as if, prior to its being, nothing existed, and only afterward something is.

Furthermore, should it be supposed that the relation to nothing implied in the proposition is positive, in this sense that for the creature to be made from nothing means to be made after nothing, the preposition 'after' implying an order absolutely. But there is order and order, namely, that of duration and that of nature. If then the proper and particular does not follow from the common and universal, it would not be necessary that from the fact that the creature is said to exist after nothing, nothing should have been prior in duration and afterward there was something. It suffices that nothing is prior to being in nature. That in a thing which belongs to it of itself is prior to what it owes to another. But existence is something the creature has only from another; considered as left to itself it is nothing. So in the creature nothing is naturally prior to existence.

It doesn't follow that nothing and being are at once from the fact that there is no priority in duration, for it is not maintained that, if the creature always was, at some time it was nothing, but rather that its nature is such that it would be nothing if left to itself. For if we were to say that the air is always illumined by the sun, we must say air had been made lucid by the sun. And because whatever comes to be, comes to be from that which does not exist simultaneously with what is said to come to be, it must be said that if it was made lucid from the non-lucid, or shady, not in the sense that it ever was non-lucid or shaded but rather because it would be if the sun deserted it. This is crystal clear in the stars and planets which are always illumined by the sun.

It is clear, then, that when something is said to have been made by God and to have never not been, there is no incoherence. If there were it is marvelous it was not seen by Augustine, since this would be a quick way to disprove the eternity of the world. But he fashioned, in the eleventh and twelfth books of *The City of God*, many arguments to disprove the eternity of the world. Why would he have omitted this one [i.e., that it is incoherent to say the world is eternal]?

Indeed he seems to imply that there is no such incoherence, for speaking of the Platonists in the tenth book, chapter 31, he writes, "How they understood this does not seem to involve time but a principle of subordination. For, they say, just as if a foot were eternally in the dust, its imprint would always be there, yet no one would doubt it had been made by the foot, yet the one would not be prior to the other even though the one is caused by the other. So too, they say, the world and the gods created in it always were, since the one making them always exists, yet they are made." He never says this cannot be understood, but proceeds otherwise against the position.

So too, in the eleventh book, chapter 4, he says, "One confessing that the world was made by God but wanting there to be no beginning in time of its creation, such that in a manner scarcely intelligible it was always made, say something indeed (and wish to defend God as it were from fortuitous rashness)." The reason it is scarcely intelligible was stated in our first argument.

It is cause for wonder then why the greatest philosophers seem unaware of the supposed incoherence. For Augustine says in the same eleventh book, chapter 5, referring to those mentioned in the previous text, "We now discourse with those who agree with us in saying that there are no bodies or natures of which God is not the creator," and later adds, "These philosophers surpass all others in nobility and authority."

Anyone thinking seriously of it then must conclude that those who held the world had always been, but at the same time said it was caused by God, are guilty of no conceptual incoherence. Those who detect this incoherence, therefore, must alone be men and wisdom first arose with them!

Since some authorities seem to support them, however, we must show how weak that support is.

St. John Damascene, in *On the Orthodox Faith*, book one, chapter 8, says, "it is not in the nature of things that what is brought from non-being to being should be coeternal with Him who is without beginning and always is."

And Hugh of St. Victor, at the beginning of *On the Sacraments*, writes, "The power of the ineffable omnipotence cannot have something beside itself and coeternal that it uses in making."

But these and similar authorities can be understood by means of what Boethius says in the *Consolation of Philosophy*, Book Five, prose 6, "They are incorrect who when they hear that Plato held that this world neither had a beginning in time nor will have an end understand him to mean that this made world becomes coeternal with its maker. For it is one thing to endure through a life unending, which is what Plato says of the world, and another to be unending life whole and presently complete, which is clearly proper to the divine mind."

So it is clear that what some maintain does not follow, namely that creatures would be equal to God in duration. So understood, nothing can be coeternal with God because only God is immutable. This is clear from Augustine, *City of God*, book twelve, chapter 15, "Time which runs on mutably cannot be coeternal with immutable eternity. Thus if the immortality of the angels does not traverse time nor have a past which no longer is nor a future which is not yet, their movements go through successive times and change from future to past. They cannot, then, be coeternal with the creator of whom we cannot say there is any movement that no longer is or future that is not yet." So too in book eight of *On Genesis Literally*, chapter 23, "The nature of the trinity is wholly immutable and for this reason is eternal in such a way that nothing can be coeternal with it." And much the same can be found in the *Confessions*, book eleven, chapter 30.

They [Thomas's adversary, the murmurers] also adopt arguments from Aristotle, among which the most difficult has to do with the infinity of souls, because if the world has always been it would be necessary that there are now souls infinite in number. But this argument is not relevant, because God could make the world without animals and souls and make man when he did, the rest of the world being eternal, and thus an infinity of souls would not arise. Besides, it has not been shown that God could not create an actual infinite.

There are other arguments I won't consider now, either because they have been dealt with elsewhere or because they are so weak that of themselves they render the opposite position unlikely.

On the Eternity of the World Against Murmurers

6. THEOLOGIAN AS PHILOSOPHER

SEVERAL TIMES you have been told that St. Thomas is a theologian. Along the way, you will have noticed that a distinction is being drawn between the philosopher and the theologian. Indeed, there is a conflict between Thomas and his theologian colleagues over the newly available philosophical works of Aristotle. Yet I persist in speaking of the philosophy and philosophical work of Thomas. You are confused. Am I?

Philosophical Assumptions

When we were contrasting what we called the Classical view with Modernity, we stressed the fact that in the classical mode in which Thomas moves, it is assumed that you bring to your study of philosophy a good many truths about the world and yourself and it is from these that the formal study of philosophy begins.

Philosophy assumes these starting points are already there. It does not presume to confer on you the possibility of having true thoughts for the first time. That presumption is characteristic of Modernity, Gnosticism, and used car salesmen.

In the classical mode of doing philosophy, anything that is proposed for your acceptance must be commended on the basis of what you already know. Philosophical discourse looks like this. Given that A and B are so, it follows that C is so. A and B are the premises, C the conclusion. The premises with which all philosophical theories must ultimately accord are already known by everybody.

If you go to the library and randomly pull a work of philosophy from the shelf, chances are that, opened even at the
first page, it will read like a foreign language, even though
it is actually in English of a sort. Proceeding otherwise than
randomly, I could cite such gems as the following to make
the point.

> Philosophy deals essentially with the general in which the par-
> ticular is subsumed. Therefore, it *seems*, more than in the case
> of other sciences, as if the aim or the final results gave expres-
> sion to the subject matter itself, even as if they did entire justice
> to its very essence, while the way in which things are worked
> out in detail may seem to be unessential . . .

> Philosophy may be said to contain the principles of the rational
> cognition that concepts afford us of things (not merely, as with
> Logic, the principles of the form of thought in general irrespec-
> tive of the Objects), and, thus interpreted, the course, usually
> adopted, of dividing it into *theoretical* and *practical* is perfectly
> sound. But this makes imperative a specific distinction on the
> part of the concepts by which the principles of this rational cog-
> nition get their Object assigned to them . . .

I do not say that you might not learn to decipher such ob-
fuscating remarks, the first from Hegel, the second from Kant,
but then you might learn Swahili too. Contrast their Teutonic
and musclebound prose with this:

> All men by nature desire to know. An indication of this is the
> delight we take in our senses; for even apart from their useful-
> ness they are loved for themselves; and above all others the sense
> of sight. For not only with a view to action, but even when we
> are not going to do anything, we prefer seeing (one might say)
> to everything else. The reason is that this, most of all the senses,
> makes us know and brings to light many differences between
> things.

That's Aristotle, beginning his most difficult work, the *Metaphysics*. You know from the very beginning what he is saying:

he is speaking your language. He is reminding us of what we already know.

Hegel and Kant, on the other hand, are addressing the initiate. They refer to quasi-technical usage that they presume known by their readers. They are writing for professionals. They would not assume that a generally intelligent reader could follow what they are writing.

In saying these things, I am not being obscurantist. I do not intend to engage in that "clerical treason" whereby the intellectual mocks his own way of life, preening himself by implying that he is not like the others. I will plead as guilty as anyone to treating philosophy as if it were the interest of a coterie and as for abusing the language, I too have sinned, *mea culpa, mea culpa, mea maxima culpa.*

Nor, of course, does a pellucid style guarantee that what is said is true. G. E. Moore and Bertrand Russell, the first always, the second when he wanted, addressed their philosophy to everyman.

Not every philosophical discussion is a threshold one, connecting in obvious ways with common experience and ordinary uses of the language. But in what we are calling Modernity, there is no desire to hook up with what everybody knows. The Classical view requires that every discussion, every truth claim, be such that we can be led back from it to those great common truths which everybody knows and which are the ultimate warrant for accepting whatever be proposed. Modernity begins with the denial that there is such a fund of commonly possessed non-gainsayable truths to which reference must always be made.

Theological Assumptions

Revealed truths are to theology what commonly known truths are to philosophy.

Just as the philosopher in the classical mode draws attention to what we all already know, makes it explicit, goes on from it, so the theologian assumes faith, belief in truths revealed by God, makes them explicit, arranges them in various ways, defends them against attack, derives other truths from those which have been explicitly revealed.

Theological discourse is pretty clearly different from philosophical, or any other, discourse. Its assumed starting points are truths which are held on the basis of divine faith. That there are three Persons in God, that Jesus is both human and divine, that He rose from the dead thus enabling us to do the same, that sins can be forgiven, that Christ founded the Church, the priesthood, the sacraments—all these, familiar as they are to believers, do not fall among the things that anybody can know on the basis of common experience of the world. If one does not hold these to be true, whatever logical connections he might see between them and the theologian's conclusions, those conclusions will not be accepted as *truths* by the nonbeliever.

Overlaps

This does not mean that the truths of faith are unrelated to what everybody knows. When Jesus wants to tell us of the mercy of God He tells the story of the Prodigal Son. The listener understands what is meant from the comparison drawn between fathers and sons, just as water and bread and wine are used sacramentally to mean cleansing from sin and spiritual food. But if common truths are appealed to in God's revealing of Himself to us, revealed truths do not follow from them as conclusions from premises.

Philosophy, as an extension of common knowledge, is presupposed by theology, in somewhat the same way as common truths are presupposed by faith. This is the origin of the description of philosophy as the handmaid or servant of theology.

The thing that struck Thomas in his study of Aristotle was that philosophers had arrived at truths about God which are equivalent to some revealed truths. We'll see later that, after recounting Aristotle's proof of the Prime Mover, Thomas will add, and that's what we mean by God. The "we" includes believers. God as the first cause of all else is known by Aristotle, Thomas says, and that is a truth we have accepted from childhood as part of our religion.

That there is only one God, that God is intelligent and good and just—these have been taught by philosophers as truths which can ultimately be derived from truths about the world and ourselves.

So there is an overlap between the theology of the philosophers and that based on Holy Scripture. Some of the things God has told us about Himself can be known apart from Revelation, derived from what is known about the world. Thomas calls these Preambles of Faith.

These are matters to which we shall return. For now, we have said enough to show the difference Thomas sees between philosophy and theology. The analogy we noticed is of great importance.

$$\frac{\text{Common Truths}}{\text{Philosophy}} : \frac{\text{Faith}}{\text{Theology}}$$

In order to do theology, one must first have done philosophy. The very first question Thomas asks in his *Summa theologiae* is: What need is there for any science other than those which make up philosophy? The question only makes sense if one knows those philosophical sciences.

In analyzing the truths of faith, truths like the Trinity, the theologian will employ such notions as nature and person and substance and will rely on what philosophers have to say on those subjects. Sometimes the theologian has to develop philosophical notions which are not available and when he does he is contributing to philosophy as well as to theology. Thomas often does this and we will add those contributions to the synthesis we call Thomistic philosophy.

The way Thomas does theology follows from his attitude

toward Aristotle. Rather than see Aristotle as a threat, Thomas studied him closely and learned an enormous amount of truth. The basic characteristic of Thomas is that there can be no real conflict between what is known and what is believed, between faith and reason, between philosophy and theology. If philosophers think they know something that is in conflict with faith, Thomas would proceed as he did with Aristotle, wanting to discuss the matter, in the conviction that something must have gone wrong in the philosophical discourse that has led to a conclusion which contradicts the faith.

The skeptic and agnostic may be annoyed by this untroubled conviction, but they can always demand that the flaw be shown.

The theologian and Christian philosopher should be ready to pay off on this sunny conviction. When philosophical positions which conflict with faith are shown to be flawed, the reasonableness of belief is made clear. Thomas's policy to the effect that this can always be done is the policy of the Church as well. Let no man think that religious faith runs from reason. As we have said before and will say again, in our day the best safeguard of reason is precisely the Christian faith.

TEXT OF THE MASTER

Knowledge of God

[1] The human intellect, to which it is connatural to derive its knowledge from sensible things, is not able through itself to reach the vision of the divine substance in itself, which is above all sensible things and, indeed, improportionately above all other things. Yet, because man's perfect good is that he somehow know God, lest such a noble creature might seem to be created to no purpose, as being unable to reach its own end, there is given to man a certain way through which he can rise to the knowledge of God: so that, since the perfections of things descend in a certain order from the highest summit of things—God—man may progress in the knowledge of God by beginning with lower things and gradually ascending. Now, even in bodily movements, the way of descending is the same as the way of ascending, distinguished by beginning and end.

[2]   There is a twofold account of the descent of perfections from God just mentioned. One account looks to the first origin of things: for divine Wisdom, to put perfection in things, produced them in such order that the universe of creatures should embrace the highest of things and the lowest. The other account comes from the things themselves. For, since causes are more noble than their effects, the very first caused things are lower than the First Cause, which is God, and still stand out above their effects. And so it goes until one arrives at the lowest of things. And because in the highest summit of things, God, one finds the most perfect unity— and because everything, the more it is one, is the more powerful and the more worthy—it follows that the farther one gets from the first principle, the greater is the diversity and variation one finds in things. The process of emanation from God

must, then, be unified in the principle itself, but multiplied in the lower things which are its terms. In this way, according to the diversity of things, there appears the diversity of the ways, as though these ways began in one principle and terminated in various ends.

[3]   Through these ways our intellect can rise to the knowledge of God. But because of the weakness of the intellect we are not able to know perfectly even the ways themselves. For the sense, from which our knowledge begins, is occupied with external accidents, which are the proper sensibles—for example, color, odor, and the like. As a result, through such external accidents the intellect can scarcely reach the perfect knowledge of a lower nature, even in the case of those natures whose accidents it comprehends perfectly through the sense. Much less will the intellect arrive at comprehending the natures of those things of which we grasp few accidents by sense; and it will do so even less in the case of those things whose accidents cannot be grasped by the senses, though they may be perceived through certain deficient effects. But, even though the natures of things themselves were known to us, we can have only a little knowledge of their order, according as divine Providence disposes them in relation to one another and directs them to the end, since we do not come to know the plan of divine Providence. If, then, we imperfectly know the ways themselves, how shall we be able to arrive at a perfect knowledge of the source of these ways? And because that source transcends the above-mentioned ways beyond proportion, even if we knew the ways themselves perfectly we would yet not have within our grasp a perfect knowledge of the source.

[4]   Therefore, since it was a feeble knowledge of God that man could reach in the ways mentioned—by a kind of intellectual glimpse, so to say—out of a superabundant goodness, therefore, so that man might have a firmer knowledge of Him, God revealed certain things about Himself that transcend the human intellect. In this revelation, in harmony with man, a certain order is preserved, so that little by little he

comes from the imperfect to the perfect—just as happens in the rest of changeable things. First, therefore, these things are so revealed to man as, for all that, not to be understood, but only to be believed as heard, for the human intellect in this state in which it is connected with things sensible cannot be elevated entirely to gaze upon things which exceed every proportion of sense. But, when it shall have been freed from the connection with sensibles, then it will be elevated to gaze upon the things which are revealed.

[5]   There is, then, in man a threefold knowledge of things divine. Of these, the first is that in which man, by the natural light of reason, ascends to a knowledge of God through creatures. The second is that by which the divine truth—exceeding the human intellect—descends on us in the manner of revelation, not, however, as something made clear to be seen, but as something spoken in words to be believed. The third is that by which the human mind will be elevated to gaze perfectly upon the things revealed.

Summa contra gentiles, Book Four, chapter 1

7. WHAT IS A THING?

FOR THOMAS there is one great division in reality, that between God and creatures. St. Paul in Romans 1.19–20 tells us that pagans can from the things that are made come to knowledge of the invisible things of God, and indeed that is the message of Aristotle as well. From the changing things of this world we can come to knowledge of the Prime Mover or God.

Things are part of a vast ordered whole, the cosmos, and it may seem that such proofs take the cosmos as effect and God as cause. Not quite. We must first get clear on what is meant by things.

It seems a funny question. The word 'thing' is so elastic in its uses that it does not seem too promising to ask for a definition. Everything is a thing and things are very diverse from one another. Let's look at the way Aristotle approached the question, because Thomas thought it right as rain and adopted it as his own.

Out of Confusion

It is all too true that the world is made up of a multitude of things, whether or not more than are dreamt of in our philosophy. Recent discussions of what there is, the things that are, predictably begin with the fear of asserting that something is, which is not. And the meaning of 'nothing' is queried. Numbers and ideas and physical objects are enumerated as kinds of things and one can get the impression that they are equally evident to us. This is the wrong kind of confusion with which to begin.

At the basis of all our knowledge is sensation. The things that exist are in the first instance what can be grasped by means of our senses. Our ideas of these things are at first vague and confused. Aristotle uses the example of something first seen at a great distance but approaching us. It's something, it's alive, it's an animal, it's human, it's my mother-in-law. All knowledge moves like that, from generality and confusion toward precision and particularity.

The first and most general way of thinking of the things that are is as products of change. The world is made up of things that have come to be as the result of a change, undergo all kinds of changes in their careers, and finally cease to be as the result of a change. To call something *physical* or *natural* is to say just that. The Greek word from which 'physical' derives means growth. Nature suggests being born. Things come to birth, that is the idea, but in this use being born is not distinguished from other ways of coming into being. Whatever comes to be as the result of a change—that is what is meant by physical or natural things.

Physical Objects

What are the first truths we can attain about physical objects? The analysis we are going to sketch is found in Book One of Aristotle's *Physics*. Before giving his own account, Aristotle surveys what others have had to say on the subject. This is important. The Classical philosopher—and no one is more representative of the tribe than Aristotle—is not interested in developing an original position. He will be guided by what others say, the many, but even more those who have reflected on the subject. At first blush, previous opinions suggest the Tower of Babel, but Aristotle finds certain common notes struck despite the diversity, and those common notes stand a good chance, he thinks, of being the truth of the matter.

It is against that background that he takes up the subject anew. What is a physical object? Something that has come to be as a result of a change. So what is change?

We need an example. Let us say you gave your nephew
Orville a mouth organ for his birthday and then got out of
town. Months later, having forgotten your unfriendly act, you
return on a visit and are pleasantly surprised to hear little Orville render *Stars and Stripes Forever* in a creditable manner.
Orville who once could not play the mouth organ now can.
This can be stated in a variety of ways.

[1] A boy becomes musical.
[2] The unmusical becomes musical.
[3] The unmusical boy becomes musical.

The three expressions of the same change have three different
grammatical subjects. Moreover, all three expressions are of
the syntactical form "*A* becomes *B.*"

Sometimes the expression of a change takes the form "From
A, *B* comes to be." So let's restate the variety in this second
form.

[4] From a boy, musical comes to be.
[5] From unmusical, musical comes to be.
[6] From the unmusical boy, musical comes to be.

Some of these sound all right, but [4] rings false. Why? Because it suggests that when skill with the mouth organ puts
in an appearance, the boy ceases to be. That is why [5] and
[6] ring true—unmusical and unmusical boy do cease to be
as a result of the change.

We can distinguish between the grammatical subject of the
sentence expressing the change and the subject of the change.
*The subject of the change is that to which the change is attributed
and which survives the change.* Something—musical—is denied
of the subject before the change and affirmed of it afterward.
The subject of the change lacks before the change what it gains
as a result of the change. The subject, a lack, and a gain—
these three elements seem true of any change. They are the
least we can say of a change and thus are true of every change.

These elements of change get names in Aristotle from another example he uses of a change in wood whereby from

unshaped or unformed it becomes shaped or formed. Using the terms to cover all examples, Aristotle speaks of wood or matter (subject) and privation (lack) and form (gain) as elements of all change.

Little Orville moves from the back yard to the front, from pale to tan, from five feet tall to six and a half and in all such changes—of place, of color, or size—we can speak of matter, privation, and form. We attribute these changes to Orville because he changes in these respects, in respect of place, color, and size. But as the subject, Orville survives the change. He does not come to be as subject in any of these changes. Yet there was a time when Orville himself was not and eventually, alas, he will be no more. What of those more dramatic changes?

Substantial Change

Do autonomous units like little Orville come into existence as the result of a change? Of course they do. No one would deny that once Orville was less than a twinkle in the parental eye yet here he is playing *Stars and Stripes Forever* on that blasted mouth organ. Would anyone deny that Orville is *something one* in as basic a sense as there is?

Sure. Some philosophers. Of course, they're wrong.

Aristotle knew of atomists who said that big things like Orville and cows and trees and your mother-in-law are not basic. They are not units so much as made up of units and finally of units that can't be cut up any further—that's what 'atom' means. Orville is a swarm of atoms which are rearranged in various ways and one rearrangement leads us to say he has grown tan, another that he has gone into the backyard, yet another that there is no more Orville to talk about.

This has been called the "Hang on to the brush, I'm taking away the ladder" form of argument. In order to know what you mean by something one, you will mention things like Orville, his uncle, the dog, and so forth. The next step is to say that they are not really ones but made up of things that are really one. The real ones, the atoms, are one in the sense derived from Orville, his uncle, the dog, and so forth. In short, if Orville isn't a unit, there is no way we can explain what is meant by calling an atom a unit.

This is not, of course, a rejection of the view that big things have smaller components and that our knowledge of big things increases as we come to know more of their components. Rather it is a good example of Aristotle's insistence that progress in knowledge is made by way of addition to what is already known, not by abstraction from or denial of it. Things which undergo change in respect of place and color and size are called substances.

The assumptions of the discussion then are two: such things as Orville and trees and dogs are fundamental natural units *and* they come to be as a result of a change.

The task is to see how what we already know of change can be used to cast light on the coming into being of substances.

Prime Matter

Substantial change is analyzed by arguing by analogy from the changes substances undergo in their qualities or accidents. The subject of the changes analyzed up until now is a substance. What is gained by the change does not make the substance to be a substance, but only to be in a certain respect, here as opposed to there, tan as opposed to pale, fat as opposed to thin. To what subject can the change thanks to which Orville comes into existence be attributed?

If any change involves a subject, privation, and form, then substantial change must do so. But if that subject is itself a substance, then to-be-Orville relates to it as to-be-tan relates to Orville. And then the change is not a substantial one, but an accidental one. The subject of substantial change must be similar, but not identical to that of accidental change. It cannot be itself a substance. To underscore this, Aristotle calls it prime matter.

Euclid alone has looked on beauty bare, if Edna St. Vincent Millay is right, but no one, least of all Aristotle, has ever seen prime matter. It is known to be on the basis of the comparison we have just traced. If there must be a subject of any change, if substances come to be as the result of a change, and they do, there must be a subject to which substantial change is attributed. That subject cannot be matter or subject in the usual sense, that is, a substance. The subject to which substantial change is attributed is thus called prime matter.

It will be noticed that Aristotle makes appeal to no special experience in this analysis. He is setting forth the implications of what anyone knows. He makes no assumptions that are not in the public domain. At the end of the analysis we know what we did not know before, but the new knowledge was implicit in what we already knew.

Moreover, prime matter is not like the atoms of the Greek atomists, although both are such that you cannot just look at them. Unlike the atoms, whose acceptance requires that we stop meaning what we say of Socrates and Fido as basic units, prime matter is recognized as the necessary condition for our ordinary talk being true. If prime matter prevented ordinary talk that would count heavily against it as it does against atomism.

Needless to say, what we have come to know by means of this analysis is of glittering generality and is hardly what we would be content with. This is the first step in natural science, not the last.

Once more we see a characteristic of what we are calling the Classical view. Certainties and clarifications need not be once and for all. Just as we can be quite clear about plane figures and not yet of the distinctions between circles and squares and triangles, just as we can get clear about triangles and still not be clear on the difference between scalene and isosceles triangles, so we can be clear on the principles of change in general and have made only a first step on a long, long trail to particular knowledge of natural kinds.

We began by identifying the physical or natural thing as that which has come to be as the result of a change. We can now say that the result of change is always a compound of matter and form. If you hear this referred to as hylomorphism, don't worry. *Hyle* is the Greek word for wood and *morphe* means shape or form, so the fancy term means only that what has come to be is shaped wood, or formed matter, or a combination of matter and form.

TEXT OF THE MASTER

The Principles of Nature

[2]   He uses the following argument to prove that there are two essential (per se) principles of nature. What natural things are and come to be from per se and not accidentally are called their principles and causes; but whatever comes to be is and comes to be from a subject and a form; therefore the subject and form are per se principles of everything that comes to be in nature.

That what comes to be in nature comes to be from subject and form is proved thus. Those things into which the definition of a thing is analyzed are that thing's components: what something is analyzed into are its components. But the account of what comes to be naturally is resolved into subject and form: for the account of musical man is resolved into the concept of musical and the concept of man, since anyone seeking to define musical man will have to provide definitions of musical and of man. Therefore what naturally comes to be is and comes to be from subject and form. . . .

[3]   Then when he [Aristotle] says *Est autem subiectum, etc.*, he adds a third accidental principle.

And he says that, although the subject is numerically one, in type and concept it is two . . . because man and gold and every matter has a certain number. We can consider the subject itself, which is something positive, from which something comes to be per se and not accidentally, like man or gold; and we can consider what inheres in it as an accident, such as contrariety and privation, e.g., unmusical, unshaped. The third principle is species or form, as its arrangement is the form of the house, and musical is the form of musical man, etc., etc.

Form and subject, then, are per se principles of what comes

73

to be naturally, but privation or the contrary is an accidental principle, as being accidental to the subject. Thus we say that the builder is the per se efficient cause, but musical is an accidental efficient cause of it insofar as the builder happens to be musical. So too, man is the per se cause, as subject, of musical man, but not-musical is its accidental cause and principle. [4]   Someone might object that privation does not inhere in the subject when it has received the form and that privation ought not therefore be called an accidental cause of *being.*

To which it can be said that matter is never without privation, because when it has one form it is deprived of another. Thus when something which comes to be, musical man, say, is in the process of becoming, the subject, insofar as it does not yet have the form musical is the privation of musical; so not-musical is an accidental principle of the coming to be of musical man. But when this form is joined to it, the subject is in privation of another form; therefore the privation of the opposite form is an accidental form of being.

It is clear that Aristotle does not mean that the privation which he holds to be an accidental principle of nature is an aptitude for form, or an inchoative form, and any sort of imperfect active principle, as some think, but the very absence of form or the contrary of the form which inheres in the subject.

Commentary on Physics, Book One, lesson 13

8. ART AND NATURE

ARTIFICIAL AS well as natural things come into being as the result of a change and in some sense art is closer to us than nature. After all, we produce artifacts. Well, artisans and artists do, but you and I know what it is like to type a page, make a paper airplane, bake a cake, so perhaps there is a sense in which we are all artists. Man is naturally an artisan; the artificial is natural to us.

Art Presupposes Nature

A natural thing is made up of matter and form and each of these components is a source of changes we attribute to it. Any natural or physical thing will, if let go of, drop. We attribute this to its matter because a man, his dog, and a geranium will all fall when dropped so we do not think this a peculiarity of humans, dogs, or geraniums. A person's laughter, on the other hand, is thought to belong to her because of the specific kind of thing she is.

Form sets a thing off from other things. This is true of form in its primary sense of shape. You can sort out the square ones and the round ones from the rectangular ones. It is because form enables us to sort things that the word for external shape was extended to mean what sets one thing off from another in terms of more than its contours. The fact that things can be distinguished by color and place led to calling these features forms too and finally what makes a thing to be a substance of this type rather than that is called its form. Natural kinds or sorts are read from form rather than matter. Nonetheless, changes due to the thing's matter as well as those due to its form will be said to be natural to it.

Its nature is that in the thing which is at the bottom of the changes it undergoes and the activities it engages in. It is intrinsic to the thing. Artificial changes, by contrast, come from outside in the sense that they require the intervention of a human being.

When a tree is felled, the wood obtained is a product of nature. Many years ago, an acorn germinated, rain fell, the sun shone, the acorn became the mighty oak that now lies fallen in the forest. Logs, insofar as they are sections of the felled tree made with saw or axe, are artificial things. Lumber is even more so. And the house built from the boards is an even more complicated artifact.

An artifact comes into being when a shape or form is imposed by a human agent on a natural material. So the artifact is composed of matter and form. In the case of logs, the matter is obviously produced by nature. When the logs are the matter from which lumber is made, we are twice removed from nature, the house yet further removed.

An artificial change presupposes a natural matter whether proximately or remotely. No nature, no art.

Remember how Aristotle brought in an example of artificial change in his analysis of physical change. In fact, the primary example of a person learning how to play a musical instrument is a tantalizingly complicated one, somehow blending the natural and artificial. Little Orville learns to play the mouth organ.

Okay. There are natural changes and there are artificial changes. The results of natural changes are physical objects and they are made up of a form and a matter. If the natural change is a substantial one, the result is a substance of which we can say, minimally, that it is composed of prime matter and the form that makes it to be a substance of this kind. The results of artificial changes are artifacts and they too are composed of matter and form, the matter being something natural, the form a shape or distinguishing character imposed by a human being.

Art Imitates Nature

If art depends on nature in this way, it is also said to imitate nature. What does this mean? Thomas like Aristotle almost always uses the term 'art' to speak of the activity of the artisan, not the fine artist. Or to speak of the military art, the art of the master builder, the art of medicine. When he says that art imitates nature, it is of such arts we should first think.

Imitation in one sense means: consciously bringing nature to its goal, aiding nature to fulfill itself. The bandage brings torn flesh together in order that nature might heal it. An art is devised to provide shelter. Nature does not equip the human species with protection against the elements and against enemies. Nature does not prompt the human species to build a habitat in the way in which robins build nests, oven birds build their dwellings, and groundhogs make their burrows.

Instead of this, nature has given man reason and the prehensile hand. That is why art is natural to us. We must fashion what other species are provided. Turtles have shells, birds have nests, foxes have holes, men must make a place to lay their head but no blueprint is given. It can be a cave, a treehouse, a castle in Spain. Art thus provides what nature does not give, though the impulse to be artful is natural to man.

The Words of the Master

Here are two passages in which Thomas remarks on art imitating nature. The first is taken from his Commentary on the *Physics* (II,1.4,n.171)

The reason art imitates nature is that knowledge is the principle of artistic activity. But all our knowledge is received through the senses from sensible and natural things. Hence our procedure in artificial things is similar to that in natural things. Natural things are imitable by art because the whole of nature is ordered to its end by an intellectual principle, and so the work of nature seems to be a work of intelligence since it proceeds in a determinate way to definite ends—and that is imitated in artistic activity.

In the preface to his Commentary on the *Politics* of Aristotle, St. Thomas says this.

Art imitates nature, as the Philosopher teaches in the second book of the *Physics*. The reason for this is that as their principles relate to one another so proportionally do their operations and effects. The principle of art-works is the human intellect, which is derived by a kind of likeness from the divine intellect, which in turn is the principle of all natural things. Necessarily then do artistic operations imitate nature and art-works imitate things that exist in nature. If then one teaching an art produces a work of art, the apprentice desiring to acquire the art should take note so that he can act in a similar way. So it is that the human intellect, which depends on the divine intellect for its intelligible light, must be informed concerning the things it makes looking to things that are naturally produced, so that it may work in like manner.

That is why the Philosopher says that if art were to make the things which exist in nature, it would act in the same way that nature does. But, of course, nature does not completely produce artifacts; it merely provides certain starting points and offers a model. Indeed, art can observe things in nature and use them to complete its own work, although it cannot produce hose natural things. From this it is clear that human reason is merely cognitive with respect to things that exist in nature, but in respect to art works it is both cognitive and productive. Hence, human sciences which deal with natural things must be speculative, while those which deal with things produced by man must be practical or operative in a way that imitates nature.

We said earlier that art is an extrinsic principle whereas nature is an intrinsic one. This may seem unhelpful if the point is only that the artisan who makes the art work is other than and extrinsic to it. The same can be said of any effecting cause of a change, natural or artificial.

It is, of course, true that natural changes and thus natural things require effecting causes which are other than and thus extrinsic to them. What is meant by the enigmatic remark is that the natural matter of the art-work does not have within itself a capacity to become the art-work. In natural change, the matter to which the effecting cause brings a new form has a capacity to receive that form. Aristotle made this point by saying that if you planted a wooden art-work, say a bed, and it grew, what would grow would be an oak, say, and not a bed.

To Sum It Up

The contrast between art and nature, the artificial and the natural, is here meant only to cast a little more light on what is meant by the natural or physical. To know how something differs from something else is to know it better, to be able to discriminate. The contrast is not, as we have been suggesting, between two wholly unrelated realms. Rather the realm of art is said to be in various ways piggy-back on nature. The ultimate source of this is that the universe as a whole is something God has made, is an art-work of God, and thus provides a vast analogy to those human incursions into the natural world whereby we reshape and fashion it for purposes of our own. That it is natural for us to do this does not mean that the artful shapes natural material takes on are natural to it, as if computers and BVD's and popsicles would show up without human ingenuity and inventiveness.

Nowadays we are very alive to the extent to which we can safely go in our technological interventions. The sense of natural limits to art is suggestive of a moral boundary. But more of that later when we speak of natural law in the moral sense.

TEXT OF THE MASTER

The Virtue of Art

I reply that art should be called nothing else than right reason about things to be made. Their good does not consist in any disposition of the human will but rather that the work that comes to be is good in itself. The artist is not praised as an artist because of the will with which he works but because of the quality of what he makes.

Art then is properly an operative habit. Nonetheless it has things in common with speculative habits because in the latter too what counts is the things they consider rather than the way will relates to them. So long as the geometer demonstrates the true, the condition of his appetitive part—whether he is happy or sad—is irrelevant, as it is with the artist, as was mentioned. Art has the note of virtue, then, in the same way as a speculative habit does. Neither art nor the speculative habit produces a good work with respect to use, which is proper to the virtue perfecting appetite, but only gives the capacity of acting well.

Summa theologiae, First Part of the Second Part, Question 57, article 3

9. CAUSES

WHAT COMES into being as the result of a change is a compound of matter and form. Some features of physical objects or natural things are true of them because of their matter, others because of their form. It is because matter and form thus explain features of things that they are called causes.

That sounds a bit odd to us, perhaps, if we have been taught to think of cause as all but synonymous with efficient cause. A cause may seem simply what initiates a process, gets it started. On reflection, however, we can see that this identification is, in its own turn, odd.

The Table of Elements is made up of constituents of things, thanks to which they behave in this or that way. A certain activity is natural to a thing because of its make-up, and elements enter into its make-up. In this sense we have been taught to think of the constituents of a thing as causes too.

Nonetheless, and not without reason, it is of efficient causes we first think when we hear talk of causes.

The efficient cause, the mover, say, is other than and extrinsic to the moved. The moved reacts the way it does to being moved because of what it is. There are intrinsic causes as well as the extrinsic moving or efficient cause. We can see that so far we have three causes, the material and formal and the efficient. But for Thomas the most important cause of all is the final cause.

That for the sake of which something is done, the end or goal, is what prompts the mover to move and thus for a form to come to be in matter. For Thomas, as for all Aristotelians, the end is the cause of the other causes.

All the causes now mentioned fall into four familiar divisions. The letters are the causes of the syllables, the material of artificial products, fire, etc. of bodies, the parts of the whole and the premises of the conclusions, in the sense of 'that from which.' Of these pairs the one set are causes in the sense of substratum, e.g., the parts, the other set in the sense of essence — the whole and the combination and the form. But the seed and the doctor and the adviser, and generally the maker, are all sources whence the change or stationariness originates, while the others are causes in the sense of the end or the good of the rest; for 'that for the sake of which' means what is best and the end of the things that lead up to it. (*Physics* II.3)

Aristotle concludes this passage with some satisfaction. "Such then is the number and nature of the kinds of cause."

Does Nature Act for an End?

The causality of the end, final causality, what is called teleology, is introduced to explain natural events. If there is any feature of Thomas's view of the world that would appear to have been replaced by later ways of understanding nature, it is teleology.

That human beings act for the sake of an end would be pretty generally admitted, although some might take this to be only a superficial remark, the real wellsprings of action being the unconscious or environment or genetics. To speak of nature as acting for an end, however, smacks of anthropomorphism.

When we speak of the function of our senses or the role of this or that organ, we are invoking purposes, ends, teleology. We do it all the time. Especially, one might say, in science. If organisms sometimes malfunction it is because they usually function as they should. But if scientists regularly invoke purpose and function, as a group they deny that they seriously intend to speak of nature as ordered to goals or ends.

It is interesting to speculate on the reasons for this insistence. Often the rejection of teleology is taken to be essential to scientific explanation. Why this should be so, however, is unclear. If full and complete accounts of natural events could be given without reference to functions and goals, a case could be made for the mandatory expulsion of teleology. But if it is smuggled in even while it is being denied, one wants to ask what the motive is.

One pretty obvious reason is that a scientific explanation is often taken to be one that excludes any reference to a first cause of nature—that is, excludes any reference to God. Certainly the divine causality could scarcely function as a specific explanation. Why is grass green? God made it so. True as that is, it is also true of every other feature of the universe. Aristotle introduces the Prime Mover—"Whom all understand to be God," as Thomas notes—to account for the realm of nature in its totality. He rejected a mechanistic view of the cosmos. He does this because he sees a stark alternative: things come about either by chance or for the sake of the end. But the natural world is the realm of regular lawlike occurrences. What comes about by chance is random, not regular. The conclusion is clear. "If then it is agreed that things are either the result of coincidence or for an end, and these [regular occurrences in nature] cannot be the result of coincidence or spontaneity, it follows that they must be for an end" (*Physics* II.8).

Coming about by Chance

In the natural order, some things always come about in the same way, others for the most part. There is a third class, as well, things which are said to come about by chance. Some events or effects are ascribed to chance as to a cause. How did it happen? By chance. Is this really an appeal to a cause or the claim that no cause should be sought?

We can think of the role of luck in human affairs to get

clear on the matter of chance in nature. From time imme-
morial men have noted the role of luck, good and bad, in
their lives. We need an example.

Fifi LaRue, seeking relief from the academic grind, decides
to play a therapeutic round of golf. When she arrives at the
first tee, she finds no one there, so she sets off alone. She bo-
geys the first and second holes and on the third, a par three,
unwisely uses a four wood and overdrives the green by twenty-
five yards, her ball disappearing into a wooded area with dense
undergrowth. Not one to let a new ball go without a search,
Fifi wades into the wild, using her wedge as a makeshift ma-
chete. Ten minutes of fruitless search go by and an annoyed
Fifi brings her club fiercely down, half burying the head in
the ground. There is a clinking sound. Curious, Fifi scrapes
away the weeds and dirt when what to her wondering eyes
should appear but a steel case. She unearths it, lashes it to
her golf cart, takes a double bogey and goes on. In the privacy of her room, she pries open the metal case. It is full of
United States gold coins. In subsequent days, despite national
coverage, no claimants come forth. Fifi is rich. How can we
explain the change from penurious to loaded?

Doesn't our narrative tell us how it came about? Fifi found
a fortune because she had the good sense to play golf. Her
errant shot on the third hole is the cause of her being in
the brush. Her anger at losing her ball causes her to strike
the ground and thus discover the buried treasure. Those are the
reasons or causes of what happened. True as that seems, we
would nonetheless note that not everyone who plays golf finds
a fortune; not everyone who overdrives a green finds buried
treasure; not every irate linkster strikes metal let alone a metal
box filled with money when he buries a club in the turf. If
these are causes of what came about, and they are, they are
causes of a very peculiar kind.

Each of these causes is aimed at some goal other than finding treasure. If Fifi had not gone golfing, had not overdriven,
had not half buried her club, she would not have found the
money. But the aim of golfing is not to find buried money,

nor is this the goal of any of the actions that enter into Fifi's round. By doing what she does for the purposes she has, she *happens* to find the money. Finding the money happens to Fifi when she is golfing. That event is related accidentally to the activity in which she is engaged for a purpose. Fifi is the accidental cause of finding the money because it is a result accidentally related to the goal she seeks. The event is, of course, rare. If student golfers are constantly coming upon buried treasure while golfing, we would speak differently of what has happened. Fifi might be surprised, but regular golfers would not be.

What is ascribed to luck is accidental to what is sought, is rare and is significant, that is, good or bad for the agent. If a cobra had fallen off a passing circus train and taken refuge in the weeds behind the third green, Fifi might have been bitten and died; her bad luck accidentally related to her golfing as was her good luck in our original story.

Being rare is not enough to qualify as a chance event. Fifi might have been out on the course with a metal detector—say she does this every evening and finds her share of lost fountain pens, pennies, and safety pins—but tonight, bonanza! Rare as this outcome may be, it is what she seeks to bring about. We would call her lucky, maybe, but the difference between this story and the original one is vast.

Chance in Nature

If nature acts for an end and not everything in nature comes about always or necessarily, there will be rare occurrences when nature fails to do what she regularly does. Some natural events will be said to come about by chance, say, a freak or monster, when nature does not achieve her aim. The aim is read from what usually happens.

Given this understanding of chance, it is no surprise that the suggestion that the world of nature can ultimately be ascribed to chance is summarily rejected. The chance event must ride piggyback on some action which intends a given end. Chance presupposes teleology and cannot replace it.

But is that what is meant by chance when someone (Monod) today says the whole shebang is due to chance? Often what is meant is statistical improbability. That life should begin is a billion (or more, much more) to one shot. However true that is, it does not settle whether life was meant to begin. It is the rare acorn that becomes an oak, it is statistically improbable, but for all that it is intended.

Surely there is no need to say that these pre-Modern features of Classical natural philosophy do not make up a rival account to natural science. The Classical philosopher, of course, assumes that there is continuity between what everyone already knows about the world around us and scientific theories. It is the rare though existent bird who holds that science is destined to replace our ordinary knowledge of the world. It is no part of the Classical view to prefer common sense to science, as if they were rivals. The assumption is that both are part of our knowledge of nature.

The notion of accidental causality is also crucial for turning aside another and more radical assault on Classical accounts of the natural world. Very early on in the efforts to understand the natural world there were those who maintained that the natural world must be an illusion since change is impossible.

TEXT OF THE MASTER

The Four Causes

From what has been said it is clear that there are three principles of nature, namely, matter, form, and privation. But these are not sufficient for generation.

What is potentially cannot make itself actual, as copper which is potentially an idol does not make itself an idol, but a workman is needed if the potential idol is to emerge into actuality. Form cannot draw itself forth from the potency of matter (I mean the form of what is generated, which we call the term of generation); form is found only in the thing once made; what acts is involved in becoming, when the thing comes to be. That is why there must be some active principle apart from form and matter and we call it the efficient or active or moving cause or that whence comes the start of motion.

Because, as Aristotle says in *Metaphysics* II, whatever acts only acts by intending something, there must be a fourth, namely that which the agent intends, and this is called the end.

Notice that, although every agent both natural and voluntary intends an end, it does not follow that every agent knows the end or deliberates about the end. Knowledge of the end is necessary when actions are not determined but can go either way, as with voluntary agents. They must know the end in order to determine their acts to it. But the actions of natural agents are determined, so they need not choose what is for the end. Avicenna gives the example of the harpist who need not deliberate about each plucking of the strings since his acts are determined by him; if not, there would be a pause between notes and a resultant dissonance. Deliberation then is a feature of voluntary rather than of natural agents. So, arguing from the greater, if the voluntary agent sometimes does not deliberate, the natural agent never will. It is possible therefore for a natural agent to intend an end without deliberating about it: to intend means nothing more than have a natural inclination to it.

It follows from all this that there are four kinds of cause, namely, the material, efficient, formal, and final.

Although Aristotle says in the *Metaphysics* that whatever is a principle is a cause and vice versa, in the *Physics* he posits four causes and three principles. Causes are both extrinsic and intrinsic. Matter and form are intrinsic to the thing in that they are the parts constituting the thing; the efficient and final are called extrinsic since they are outside the thing. Only intrinsic causes are called principles. Privation is not included among the causes because it is an accidental principle, as has been pointed out. When we say there are four causes we mean per se causes, to which accidental causes are reduced, because the accidental is always reduced to the essential.

On the Principles of Nature, chapter 3

10. PARMENIDES' PROBLEM

NO SOONER had the effort to understand the natural world begun than a huge obstacle was put in the way of continued inquiry. What the various ways of understanding natural becoming had in common, needless to say, was the assumption that there were things coming into being.

Parmenides, a formidable thinker, made a disturbing point. Becoming entails that something that had not previously existed comes into being. That is, being is the result of becoming. If being is the end term of becoming, where does it start? Where does the new being come from? Parmenides saw only two possibilities.

[1] Being comes from being.

[2] Being comes from non-being.

If these terms-from-which indeed exhaust the possibilities, becoming is impossible, because being can come from neither being nor non-being. If being becomes being (or, to put it another way, if being comes from being), we have the same thing before and after the change. But then there is no change. If, on the other hand, we say that non-being becomes being (or being comes from non-being), we are saying in effect that nothing comes to be. That is, the nothing is the subject of the change and survives it. But that is a denial of change, rather than its assertion.

The Parmenidean point can be stated in terms of a denial of plurality. In order to speak of change, we must have the thing that was and the thing that now is, two things. If they are two, they must differ. There are two ways in which A differs from B, either in being or in non-being. But if we say that the first being differs from the second being in being, this is no difference. If we take the remaining option and say the two beings differ in non-being, this is to say they differ in nothing. They are one and the same.

No matter how you slice it, Parmenides concluded, change is impossible. Oh, we think we see many things and we think they are undergoing changes, but if change resists any coherent analysis, we must conclude that our senses are deluding us. Whatever we think we see, we *know* that being is one, unique, unchanging.

Being and Appearance

For the first time in the history of philosophy we have theory urged against experience, mind over matter, alleged being over deceptive appearance. We cannot believe our eyes because if we did we would have to think the unthinkable: that nothing becomes something.

In reading what Parmenides said you will have the distinct impression that your leg is being pulled. You are right. But how to answer him? The history of efforts to speak of the natural world during the period between Parmenides and Aristotle is a sad one. People tried to speak of the world of becoming without running afoul of Parmenides. They wanted to acknowledge change without allowing that anything new came into being. The ancient atomic theory will suffice as an example.

There are four really real things, fire, air, earth, and water. Observable things are merely arrangements of these elements. The elements themselves do not come into being; they are simply rearranged. In Aristotelian terms, this means that all change is accidental change. Substances do not come to be. That is why the atomist can claim that his theory does not claim that any new being becomes, any new substantial being, that is.

The price paid for this is rather high. Cows and horses and

people are not substances. When a human person comes to
be this is explained simply in terms of a new arrangement
of elements which alone are being in the full sense. So a human would relate to elements as we might think color relates
to the colored thing. But if people aren't real things, we would
be hard pressed to mention what is. The ancient atomic theory thus denies that things anyone would call substances are
substances and denies substantial change as well.

What Went Wrong?

One of the merits of Aristotle's analysis of change is that
it enables us to see where Parmenides has gone wrong. Remember that Aristotle's account requires a subject and a privation in the subject of the form acquired in the change.
Before the change, the subject has a form contrary to that
acquired. Water is cold and becomes hot; the apple is green
and becomes red. Thus, before the change, the subject has
the form it has and does not have the form it will have as
the result of the change. That is why the subject is said to
be in privation of the form to be acquired. Obviously there
is an infinity of forms it does not have.

The second reminder has to do with the way in which an
activity can be attributed to an agent. Thinking of an earlier
story about Fifi LaRue, we might say

[3] The student golfs.

The statement is true. The activity of golfing can truly be attributed to the student Fifi. But we might also say

[4] The golfer golfs.

What is the difference between [3] and [4]? It happens to be
true that a student golfs, it is not part of the job description
of a student to golf—we live in a fallen universe—but when
a golfer golfs this is exactly what a golfer is supposed to do.
Let us then say that [3] happens to be true, is true *per acci-*

dens, whereas [4] is true *per se*. We saw [3] is true *per accidens* because it just happens that the same person is both a student and a golfer, and it is this happenstance connection that makes [3] turn out true.

With this as background, it is possible to deal with Parmenides. How is

[1] Being becomes being

to be understood?

If we ask ourselves how this claim can be restated in terms of Aristotle's analysis of change, we will identify the being before the change and the being after the change as, respectively, the form the subject has before the change, and the form the subject has afterward. Before the change the water is cold, afterward warm. Then [1] can be rewritten as

[1a] Cold becomes warm.

Prior to becoming warm the subject is not warm, is subject of the privation non-warm. Then we can rewrite [2] as

[2a] Not-warm becomes warm.

Both of these sentences are true, but both are true in the way [3] is, that is, *per accidens*. What Parmenides did was to understand them as *per se* attributions and he was right to see something wrong.

Why? That to which a change is attributed *per se* survives the change and is a constituent of the result. Neither cold nor not-warm survives the change whereby water becomes warm. That is why the change can be attributed to them only *per accidens*.

Potential Being

To what is the change attributed *per se*? Well, what survives the change as a constituent of the result? The subject. The water's potential to be warm is actuated by the change.

Prior to the change, when the water is cold, it has the potential to become warm. After the change, it is actually warm. That to which the change is attributed *per se* is potential being, the subject which can have the new form. This terminology comes to the fore in the definition of motion.

TEXT OF THE MASTER

Solving Parmenides' Problem

[4]   First he says that it doesn't much matter whether we say that something comes to be from being or non-being or that being or non-being does something or has something done it. And so too with the physician, whether we say that the physician does something or has something done to him or that something is or comes to be from the physician.

But to say either that the physician does something or has something done him or that something comes to be from the physician can be understood in two ways and the same applies to saying from being or non-being something comes to be or that being or non-being do or have something done them. As a matter of fact we can substitute any terms, saying, for example, that something comes to be from white or that white does or has something done to it.

That there is indeed a twofold sense of such expressions he shows in this way.

We say that the physician builds but he does not do this insofar as he is a physician, but insofar as he is a builder; so too we say that the physician comes to be white, but not insofar as he is a physician but insofar as he is black. On the other hand, we say that the physician heals insofar as he is a physician. We say the physician properly or per se does or has something done to him or that something comes to be from the physician when this is attributed to the physician as physician, per accidens, when it is attributed to him, not insofar as he is a physician, but insofar as he is something else. Thus it is clear that when it is said that the physician does or has something done to him, or that something comes to be from the physician, it can be understood in two ways, either per se or per accidens.

Manifestly then when something is said to come to be from non-being, this could be understood properly and per se if something comes to be from non-being as non-being, and so too with being.

Not grasping this distinction, the ancients erred and held that nothing comes to be and thought that nothing but what they gave as the first material principle had substantial being. For example, those saying air is the first material principle said that everything else was accidental being; in this way they excluded all substantial generation, leaving only alteration, and, because nothing can come to be per se from either being or non-being, they thought nothing could come to be from either being or non-being.

[5]   But we too say that nothing comes to be absolutely or per se from non-being, but only accidentally, because what is, that is, being, is not per se from privation. And this because privation does not enter into the essence of the thing made: a thing comes to be per se from that which is in the thing after it is made, as the shaped does not come to be per se from the unshaped, but accidentally, because after it is shaped, the unshaped is no longer in it. But this is a marvelous manner for something to come to be from non-being, one that seemed impossible to the ancient philosophers. But thus it is clear that a thing comes to be from non-being, not per se, but accidentally.

Similarly, when it is asked whether a thing comes to be from being, it should be answered that something comes to be accidentally not per se from being. . . .

[6]   Some being comes to be from not being this, but it happens that what is not this is a being. Thus something does not come to be per se from being, nor per se from non-being, coming to be per se from non-being meaning that it comes to be from non-being as non-being, as has been said.

Commentary on Physics, Book One, lesson 14

11. MOTION

SINCE NATURE is a principle of change or motion, one cannot know what nature is without knowing what motion is. To give an account of motion without introducing motion into the account is difficult. You may think this account has already been given, but this is not so. True, the analysis of the result of becoming and the Parmenidiean problem give us the elements we need for defining motion. But that task still lies ahead. Let us take it up.

The definition St. Thomas accepts from Aristotle presupposes recognition that being is divided into the potential and the actual as well as into substance and the features or accidents of substance. The category of relation is of peculiar importance since the moved is related to the mover.

The Definition

A thing can be completely actual, a thing can be only potentially, and a thing can be in between these two extremes. Something in potency alone is not moving and what is completely actual has already moved. The batter standing at home plate *could* be at first, he is potentially there. Safely on first, he has fully realized that potentiality. On the way to first, the batter is between the state of pure potentiality and that of pure actuality. Motion is the middle state, an imperfect actualization of a potency.

Looking toward home, motion is an incomplete or imperfect realization of the potency. But that alone could cover

97

the runner if he trips and falls on the way to first. So too, if we stress the potentiality still unrealized, looking toward first, this too alone covers the arrested, fallen player. How then put it? *Motion is the act of being in potency insofar as it is in potency.*

Motion is an act. An act or actuality is correlative to a potency. The full actualization of the potency is the term of the change. Motion is an imperfect act of the potency.

> Hence it is not the potency of something existing in potency nor is it the act of something actually existing, but it is the act of something existing in potency, such that by 'act' the order to the previous potency is designated and by 'existing in potency' the order to further act is designated. (*Physics* III.2.284)

The definition thus avoids invoking motion or an equivalent in defining motion, but employs the contrast between being able to be something and actually being something, a contrast everybody understands and can give examples of without hesitation. When we first read the definition, it looks like something very abstruse and difficult to understand. But if we say that motion is the act of a player who can be on first insofar as he can be on first, we can see, as Thomas says, that 'act' picks out the fact that the ability he had at home plate is no longer just pure potentiality, and 'insofar as he can be' indicates that the one whose act motion is has motion insofar as he still is in potency to be on first.

You may still object that you know perfectly well what motion is but this account of it seems very obscure. It is true *that* anyone and everyone recognizes that change occurs, knows that motion is, but this is not to be clear as to *what* it is. It is because we can easily get clear as to what potential and actual are that we can use them to express what motion is.

It is because motion and change so obviously are, because we are unlikely to doubt that they occur, that the difficulty of the account or definition of motion surprises us. The real difficulty lies in the fact that motion is such a fleeting reality, it is imperfect being. The mind more easily seizes on what is actual. No wonder the attempt to capture motion seems somewhat tortured.

But note this well. The definition commends itself in terms of what anybody already knows. That is how to appraise it. No appeal is being made to some special "philosophical" experience. 'Actual' and 'potential' should not be regarded as technical Aristotelian terms. They are no more technical than our ability to see the difference between 'could be' and 'is.'

Motion is found in a number of different categories of being: in quality, when a thing alters in quality; in quantity, when a thing changes in size or weight; in place, when a thing changes location. The change whereby a substance as such comes to be or passes away is not a motion. But more on that later.

Thomas formulates this argument on behalf of the definition. "An act is properly the act of that in which it is always found; motion is always found in something existing in potency; so motion is the act of that which exists in potency." It is the second premise he thinks needs comment.

What is actually hot is potentially cold and vice versa. Subjects like this act on one another with changes going in opposite directions. While what is hot and becoming cold is in potency to being cold, what is cold and becoming hot is in potency to being hot. This mutual interaction can be made as general as the cosmos if we say that there is one common or prime matter in every physical thing. With respect to the ultimate subject, any substance which is actually what it is, is potentially any of the other perfections or acts of matter.

Change thus looks reciprocal. What changes is changed by what it changes. The warming agent is cooled and cooling agent is warmed. Does this mean that every mover is moved? That this cannot be universally true, that there must be some mover that is not itself moved, is one of the crucial claims of Aristotle's *Physics*. This is his proof of a Prime Mover.

Whose Motion?

The recognition of reciprocal changing indicates the connection between this discussion and that on causes. Motion is the act of the moved, of that which is in potency as such, but we must relate motion to the mover as well.

Whatever at one time is only potentially and later is actual has changed. But a thing is sometimes a mover only potentially and later actually moves. Such a mover, then, is the subject of change or motion.

Whatever can be said to be at rest can be in motion, because motion and rest are opposites. But when something stops moving something, it is said to be at rest. So the mover must be subject to motion. But motion or change does not belong to the mover as mover, but rather because it moves by contact with the moved. The mover is not moved insofar as it is a mover, but insofar as it is also movable. It just happens that the mover is also moved. The mover is not moved insofar as it is a mover, but the moved is the subject of motion as such, per se.

Motion is from the mover and in the moved, speaking per se.

These clarifications turn out to be of crucial importance for the philosophical outlook that Thomas Aquinas adopts from Aristotle. If motion is the act of the moved, it requires a mover. Whatever is moved is moved by another. Is every mover in turn moved? If there is required an unmoved mover, and if moved movers are such because of sharing a matter with their effects, the unmoved mover will be free of matter.

That further importance of the definition of motion justifies our devoting time to it here.

A TEXT OF THE MASTER

The Definition of Motion

[3]   It has been pointed out that every genus is divided by act and potency. Since they are among the primary differences of being, act and potency are naturally prior to motion and the Philosopher uses them in order to define motion.

It should be considered that something is in act alone or something is in potency alone or it is midway between potency and act. What is in potency alone does not yet move; what is in complete act is not moved but has been moved. Therefore that which moves is midway between pure potency and act, and is indeed partly potential and partly actual, as is clear from alteration. For when water is only potentially hot, it is not yet moved; when it has been heated, its being heated is done, but when it has something of heat, though only imperfectly, then it is moved toward heat; for what is being heated little by little has more and more heat. The imperfect act of heat existing in the heatable is motion, not indeed insofar as it is act alone, but insofar as, according to the act it already has it is ordered to further act. If this order to further act were taken away, however imperfect its actuality, it would be the term of motion, and not motion, as happens when something is lukewarm. The order to further act belongs to that which is in potency to it.

Similarly, if the imperfect act were considered only as ordered to further act, and it compares to that further act as potency, it would not have the mark of motion but of the beginning of motion. Heating can begin from the lukewarm as well as from the cold.

Thus it is that imperfect act has the mark of motion, both insofar as it compares to further act as potency and insofar as it compares to something less perfect as act.

Therefore it is neither a potency of something existing in potency nor the act of something existing in act, but the act of something existing in potency. By 'act' the order to the previous potency is designated, and by 'of something existing in potency' the order to further act.

The Philosopher thus defines motion most properly when he says that motion is the *entelechy*, that is, *the act of something existing in potency insofar as it exists in potency.*

Commentary on Physics, Book Three, lesson 2

12. CREATION

THOMAS AS a Christian holds that the world and time had a beginning. Aristotle holds the opposite; indeed, he dismisses as ridiculous the claim that the whole realm of motion could have begun.

As we have seen, this is one of those "errors of Aristotle" that led so many of Thomas's contemporaries to see pagan philosophy as a threat. And they have a case.

Let P stand for the claim "The world had a temporal beginning" and $-P$ for the claim "The world did not have a temporal beginning." This is contradictory opposition of the first water. Only one of these can be true, and that means that the other is false. Thomas holds P, Aristotle holds $-P$. If Thomas is right, Aristotle is in error. If Aristotle is right, Thomas and all Christians, Jews, and Muslims are in error.

One of the cliches of our own day is that Aristotle denied that the world is created, Thomas, of course, held that it was, and therefore a chasm opens between the two men that can never really be bridged by Thomas's undeniable respect for Aristotle. This received opinion, like the fears of Thomas's contemporaries, fails to benefit from the distinctions Thomas himself made.

Or did he? In a famous passage, Thomas sums up the views of Plato and Aristotle in this way.

> Some progressed further and used their mind to distinguish substantial form from prime matter which they held to be uncreated; they perceived transformation to come to be in bodies with respect to essential forms, of which transformation they posited some universal causes, the ellipsis according to Aristotle, the Ideas according to Plato (*Summa theologiae* Ia.44.2).

That makes it look as if prime matter escapes the divine causality, is uncreated, and is thus a principle rivaling God himself. But Thomas goes on.

> Some advanced to consider being as such and asked after the cause of things, not only insofar as they are such and such, but insofar as they are beings. What is the cause of things insofar as they are beings is their cause not only insofar as they are of a certain kind thanks to accidental forms, nor insofar as they are of this or that kind thanks to substantial forms, but also everything else pertaining to their being in any way whatsoever.

Is Thomas excluding Aristotle from that latter group? Let's find out.

Motion Cannot Begin

The way Aristotle poses the question relies on a distinction between being at rest and being in motion. He asks if there was a time when everything was at rest, nothing in motion, and then motion began? And he answers in the negative.

He has defined motion as the act or fulfillment of the movable insofar as it is movable. Motion thus presupposes the presence of the things that are capable of motion. The subject which is in potency is presupposed, and this means either the substance which can have a different quality or quantity or place or the ultimate subject, prime matter, which can receive another essential form. Change presupposes a subject. If we say that prior to all change that which is capable of change is at rest, then there must have been an earlier change, because rest is opposed to motion. Indeed, rest is the privation of motion.

A Christian like Thomas looking at this passage in the *Physics* will put it this way. Every change presupposes a subject and what comes to be comes to be from that subject. Indeed, the subject is that to which the change is attributed. If this is true, then it is impossible for something to come to be from nothing. Wasn't this what Parmenides said? How can you attribute change to nothing? But that things came to be from nothing is precisely what we believe. It looks, then, as if our belief not only contradicts Aristotle but that creation *ex nihilo* makes no sense.

The passages we quoted earlier are from the First Part of the *Summa theologiae*. Later, commenting on the *Physics*, Thomas said this. (It seems worthwhile to quote him at length. He is more intelligible than any paraphrase of mine could be.)

It is clear that any particular active power presupposes matter, which is produced by a more universal cause, as the artisan uses the matter nature provides. But from the fact that every particular agent presupposes a matter it does not itself produce, we should not think that the first universal agent, which is causative of all being, presupposes anything which would not have been caused by him.

Nor indeed is this Aristotle's meaning. For he proves in *Metaphysics* II that that which is maximally true and maximally being is the cause of the being of all other existents. Hence, to be in potency, which is the mark of prime matter, is derived from the first principle of being, which is maximal being. Nothing need be presupposed to its action which is unproduced by it.

Since every motion requires a subject, as Aristotle here proves and as is true, it follows that the universal production of being by God is neither motion nor a change, but is a simple emanation. That is why 'become' and 'make' are equivocally common to this universal production of things and other productions.

If then we understand the production of things to be from God eternally, as Aristotle and some Platonists do, far from being necessary, it is impossible, that some unproduced subject be presupposed by this universal production. So too, if according to the teaching of our faith we hold that He did not produce things from all eternity, but produced them after they were not, it is not necessary to hold there is a subject of this universal production. (*Physics* VIII.2.974)

Aristotle's claim that every change presupposes a subject

does not conflict with a belief in a creation from nothing, that is, a production which does not presuppose any preexisting subject of the change. What is clear is that that universal production of things can be called a change only equivocally.

Thomas thus takes what initially seems to conflict with the faith as an occasion to distinguish creation from change in the usual sense, which presupposes a subject. All creation presupposes is an agent who can produce the total being of the effect.

Creation in Time

This may seem tricky. What had seemed to be a rejection of the Christian belief in creation is turned into a clarification of the way creation differs from change. But isn't Aristotle saying that change is all there is, there is no such thing as creation?

This is tantamount to another question. Does Aristotle hold that there is some first principle on which all else depends? That Aristotle holds that matter and motion have always been is clear enough. What is not clear is whether that answers the question.

Thomas wrote a little polemical work called "On the Eternity of the World Against Murmurers." It casts a great deal of light on the matter before us.

If the question asked is whether anything can exist eternally apart from the divine causality, both believer and philosopher will answer no. Like the believer, the philosopher would consider it an "abominable error" to say otherwise. Everything that is is caused by that which maximally is. This is a philosophical tenet which, as we have seen, Thomas ascribes to Aristotle. That there should be two things, God and the world, both eternally existent but having no relation to one another of cause and effect, makes no sense. If that isn't crystal clear at the moment, fear not. We will be coming back to it later.

Is it thinkable that something be at one and the same time

caused by God and exist from all eternity? Thomas wants to know if there is conceptual incompatibility between the two, such that whatever is caused by God is not eternal and whatever is eternal is not caused by God. If there is such incompatibility, it will of course be false to speak of an eternal created being. On the other hand, if an eternal created being is possible, then God could create it. What Thomas wishes to show is that it is not self-contradictory to say that something owes its existence to God with respect to all that it is and that there is no beginning to its duration.

If there were a self-contradiction, this would be due to one of two things being true or their both being true: (1) an efficient cause must precede its effect in duration; (2) non-being must precede being in duration. There are created causes which do not antedate their effects, as the sun does not exist and then there are illuminated things. Why then maintain that the creator must precede his effects in duration? Because unlike the sun he must act freely? But he is free to create from all eternity, so freedom does not seem a constraint.

The second looks tougher. If things are said to be created *ex nihilo*, this seems to require that before they exist there is nothing, and that thus non-being precedes being in duration. But the nothing from which things are created is not a previous state of affairs or a subject which could be something but at the moment is nothing. What then does it mean? "That a creature should exist it has from another; left to itself it would be nothing: hence nothing is by nature prior to existence in it." This analogy occurs to Thomas: the sun might always illumine an object, but left to itself it [the object] would not be illuminated. So its being in darkness is naturally prior to its being illuminated whether or not there was ever a time when it was not illuminated.

No wonder then that neither Augustine nor the great philosophers saw any contradiction here. Thomas adds that if we examine closely the doctrine of those who held that the world has always been, we find that they nonetheless held that the world is God's effect.

Saving Aristotle?

There is no reason to think that Thomas was out to save Aristotle at all costs, especially if the cost was an accurate rendition of what Aristotle wrote and meant. He saw himself as differing from Aristotle in maintaining, on the basis of revelation, that the duration of the world had begun. He rejects the view of those who maintained that an eternally created world is conceptually incoherent. Whether or not the world has always been, it has been created from nothing. Aristotle was right to say that the world of change and motion could not itself come into being as the result of a change. But that does not prevent its having come into being in a different way, that is, without presupposing a potential subject, something that could be but is not yet the world.

If it is true that the duration of the world began, we know this thanks to revelation. Aristotle held that the duration of the world had never begun. This is a coherent claim but false. But it is false on a basis unavailable to Aristotle, namely, revelation, so it is no defect of Aristotle's account that he did not think the world's duration was finite. Thomas understands Aristotle to be saying that the world has always been and has always been dependent on the first principle of being, maximal being.

His contemporaries accused Thomas of Aristotelianizing the faith; later he was accused of baptizing Aristotle. If he had done either, it would have been unconsciously. The fact is he did neither. He read Aristotle closely and expressed what he had read. The upshot is no surprise to him. Good philosophy and the faith are not at odds.

TEXT FROM THE MASTER

That God Brings Things into Being from Nothing

[1]   Now, what has been said makes it clear that God brought things into being from no preexisting subject, as from a matter.

[2]   For, if a thing is an effect produced by God, either something exists before it, or not. If not, our assertion stands, namely, that God produces some effect from nothing preexisting. If something exists before it, however, we must either go on to infinity, which is impossible in natural causes, as Aristotle proves in *Metaphysics* II, or we must arrive at a first being which presupposes no other. And this being can be none other than God Himself. For we proved in Book I that God is not the matter of any thing; nor, as we have shown, can there be anything other than God which is not made to be by Him. It therefore follows that in the production of His effects God requires no antecedent matter to work from.

[3]   Every matter, furthermore, is limited to some particular species by the form with which it is endowed. Consequently, it is the business of an agent limited to some determinate species to produce its effect from preexisting matter by bestowing a form upon it in any manner whatsoever. But an agent of this kind is a particular agent; for causes are proportionate to their effects. So, an agent that necessarily requires preexistent matter from which to produce its effect is a particular agent. Now, it is as the universal cause of being that God is an agent, as we proved in the preceding chapter. Therefore, in His action He has no need of any preexisting matter.

[4]   Again. The more universal an effect is, the higher its proper cause; for the higher the cause, to so many more things does its power extend. But to be is more universal than to be moved, since, as the philosophers also teach, there are some

beings—stones and the like—which are immobile. So, above the kind of cause which acts only by moving and changing there must exist that cause which is the first principle of being, and this, as we have proved in the same place, is God. Thus God does not act only by moving and changing. On the other hand, every agent which cannot bring things into being except from preexisting matter, acts only by moving and changing; for to make something out of matter is the result of some kind of motion or change. Therefore, to bring things into being with preexisting matter is not impossible. Hence, God brings things into being without preexisting matter.

[11]   The first existent, furthermore, is necessarily the cause of the things that exist; for, if they were not caused, then they would not be set in order from that first being, as we have just shown. Now, the order that obtains between act and potentiality is this: although in one and the same thing which is sometimes in potentiality and sometimes in act, the potentiality is prior in time to the act, which however is prior in nature to the potentiality. Nevertheless, absolutely speaking, act is necessarily prior to potentiality. This is evident from the fact that a potentiality is not actualized except by a being actually existing. But matter is only potentially existent. Therefore, God who is pure act, must be absolutely prior to matter, and consequently the cause of it. Matter, then, is not necessarily presupposed for His action.

[12]   Also, prime matter in some way is, for it is potentially a being. But God is the cause of everything that is, as was shown above. Hence, God is the cause of prime matter—in respect to which nothing preexists. The divine action, therefore, requires no preexisting matter.

[13]   Holy Scripture confirms this truth, saying, "In the beginning God created heaven and earth" (Gen. 1:1). For to create means nothing else than to bring something into being without any preexisting matter.

[14]   This truth refutes the error of the ancient philosophers who asserted that matter has no cause whatsoever, for they perceived that in the actions of particular agents there

is always an antecedent subject underlying the action; and from this observation they assumed the opinion common to all, that from nothing, comes nothing. Now, indeed, this is true of particular agents. But the ancient philosophers had not yet attained to the knowledge of the universal agent which is productive of the total being, and for His action necessarily presupposes nothing whatever.

Summa contra gentiles, Book Two, chapter 16

Creation is Neither Motion nor Change

[5]   Furthermore, motion or change must precede that which results therefrom; for in the being of the made lies the beginning of rest and the term of motion. Every change, then, must be a motion or a terminus of motion, which is successive. And for this reason, what is being made is not; because so long as the motion endures, something is coming to be, and is not; whereas in the very terminal point of motion, wherein rest begins, a thing no longer is coming to be; it is. In creation, however, this is impossible. For, if creation preceded its product, as does motion or change, then some subject would have to be prior to it; and this is contrary to the nature of creation. Creation, therefore, is neither a motion nor a change.

Summa contra gentiles, Book Two, chapter 17

Everything Is from God

I answer that it must be said that whatever in any way is is from God. For if something is found to be shared by a thing, it is necessary that it be caused in it by that to which it belongs essentially, as iron is ignited by fire. It was shown above, in speaking of the divine simplicity, that God is subsistent existence (*ipsum esse per se subsistens*). Again, it was shown that there can only be one subsistent existence: just as if white-ness were subsistent, it would have to be unique since white-nesses are multiplied by their recipients. It follows that things other than God are not their existence, but share in existence. Therefore it is necessary that all the things which are diver-sified because of their different ways of sharing in existence, such that they are more or less perfectly, be caused by the First Being who most perfectly exists. That is why Plato said unity must be asserted prior to any multitude. And Aristotle said in *Metaphysics* II that what is fully being and fully true is the cause of every being and every truth, as the hottest is the cause of all heat.

Summa theologiae, First Part, Question 44, article 1

13. SOUL

IF YOU were asked whether or not you are alive, the fact that you can understand and respond to the question would be a sound basis for an affirmative answer. To be alive is to be able to hear, see, feel, think, want, dream, move about, grow, and the like. This suggests levels and degrees of vital operations.

Before they send you off to the morgue, they will check you for some of the more basic vital signs we listed. And some more sophisticated ones as well, murmuring about "brain death." In keeping with our preferred procedure—it is at once Aristotelian and natural—we will be content with obvious instances.

The mirror held to the mouth of the ailing person is meant to catch a sign of life. If it clouds, there is breath, and where there is still breath we have not yet inherited. Breath. Wind. The Greeks took their word for the principle of life from that. *Psyche.* It becomes *anima* and *spiritus* and in English *Soul.*

The associations of words with psych- as their prefix, to say nothing of the movie *Psycho,* are unhelpful, and "soul" will have for most of us religious overtones. The soul is what Jesus saves, as Scripture and a host of highway signs assure us. Psychic research will suggest the slightly wacky, and talk of psychological phenomena seems meant to whisk us off to some strange and separate conceptual landscape. In reaction to that, many spend their lives proving that life is no different from other natural events. That is a healthy if mistaken conviction.

113

The Experience of Life

St. Thomas in his theological writings makes use of what Aristotle, and others, have had to say about the human soul, but such passages may not convey well the philosophical setting in which talk of the soul arises. That context is natural philosophy, that is, the effort to understand the sensible things around us. A first analysis of them as natural or physical things led to the realization that, as products of change, they are complex, a subject and a form. That is true of all natural things, though admittedly it does not tell us much about any of them specifically, however concrete and accessible the examples. Some natural things are living, others are not.

How do we know that? How do we know we are alive? Thomas does not hesitate to say that we experience in ourselves that we have a soul and that it is by the soul that we live. A soul? It is easy to imagine objectors trying to get the floor to deny that they have any such experience. They are not aware of any soul within themselves, some mysterious engine, utterly unlike any other natural thing. . . .

We cut off the microphone and with it the threat of profanity. Such objections are stimulated by many things, none of them particularly relevant to the current effort. I am tempted to suggest that we forget for the moment everything we have ever heard of spirit and soul and psyche. Think instead of breath. Breathing is a sign of life. A hard tackle can knock the wind out of an opponent and immobilize him. Announcers speak in hushed tones until they can say, "I saw him move." If what is seen is not a final twitch, we all conclude that the split end will live to catch another pass. The trainer will ask the recovered player questions to see if he is all right. His ability to say where he is, like breathing and movement, is taken to be a sign of life. Some of these signs are intermittent, and we do not consider something that has in the past and will in the future talk but cannot at the moment to be no longer among the living.

Soul is the principle of vital activities.

That's all that it is for our present purposes. Furthermore, the difference between living and nonliving natural things is a deep one. It is not superficial, like being heavy or light, here or there, large or small. To be alive is not accidental to a subject or substance. Some substances are essentially living, others not.

But can't we say that some natural things happen to be alive and others happen not to be? We just did. But when we do we don't mean that Socrates or a horse or a carrot are living things because there is a substance which from not being Socrates now happens to be Socrates, a substance which from not being a horse now happens to be a horse, and so with carrot. Why don't we mean that?

When Socrates comes to be, a new substance comes into existence. When Socrates ceases to be, a substance goes out of existence. Socrates as such is a living thing. So when he comes to be, a living substance comes to be. A dead horse is not a horse in a new state of affairs. What is referred to as a horse is no longer a horse. If someone sold him to you you would not agree you had purchased an odd sort of horse. What you have is no horse at all. It is no longer a substantial unit. Absent its principle of life, it will rapidly reveal that it is one only as a pile of things is one.

That is what we mean by denying that to be alive is accidental to a substance. There is no same thing, no permanent substantial unit, which is sometimes alive and sometimes not. The living thing is a substantial unit.

It all comes down to being able to identify some natural or physical objects as alive and others as not alive. Educated as we have been, we will have been told of species which seem difficult to classify as animals or plants, and plants which seem to fade away into the realm of the nonliving. Is crystal formation a sign of life? How very obscure it can all become, and so quickly.

Indeed it can. All the more reason to cling to the certain, to Thomas's remark that each of us has the experience of life and that the soul is that whereby he lives.

Is Thomas referring to some private and incommunicable experience, some introspective certainty over which we could quarrel endlessly? Why not put it on the basis of objective, observed happenings? But then we are going to confront puzzles about viruses and crystals and the like. As Charles De-Koninck remarked, the beauty of St. Thomas's base is that it combines the inner and the outer.

Having been struck by a Mack truck, I am carried to the hospital where I come hazily back to consciousness and hear the anxious voices of my heirs asking if I am still among the living. I lift a hand and waggle my fingers, casting gloom over the assembly. The old man is still alive.

What this gathering of eagles sees is a distinguished and despite his injuries still prepossessing old gentleman waggle his fingers. An objective experience, in the jargon we are accepting. From my supine vantage point I also observe my waggling fingers but I also am aware that I am causing that movement. Not only do I see the vital movement, I sense that I bring it about. That is when I cannot fail to know with certainty that I am alive. When I see similar activities in others I reasonably conclude that they too are alive, but it may well be that talking about it provides the surest bridge. Our conviction that there are other minds resides on the firm foundation of waggling fingers, breathing, pushing when shoved, and the like.

The Soul

The soul is that whereby we primarily live, perceive, and think—primarily because of what we said above about living substances. To be alive is not an accident of a substance. Soul cannot be an accidental form. It is, then, a substantial form.

We can now link up with things said earlier. When a natural substance comes to be, a subject which is not itself a substance, prime matter, receives a new form. If the subject were a substance, the new form would be an accidental form. The substance is that to which the change is attributed and which survives the change. Such a substance would happen to be alive as it happens to be tan.

That cannot be because when the living thing Socrates comes to be, a new substance comes to be, and when he dies, a substance is no more. The soul then is the substantial form of the living thing.

It is important to see that soul is a special kind of substantial form and that knowledge of it emerges from an analysis of change. We are in the realm of natural philosophy.

But what does it mean to say that knowledge of it arises from an analysis of change, if as we spent some time asserting there is an immediate and irrefragable certainty of life? Certainty is not always clarity. That I am sure I am alive is as true as can be, but this does not mean I know what life is. The analysis mentioned is a first step on the way to understanding what life is. We were certain of being alive long before we had any theory about life and, to repeat an earlier point, our certainty survives the theory, or so much the worse for the theory. It is not in the cards that we will end up saying there is no difference between what we initially called living and what we initially called nonliving. The theory is meant to account for this difference, not eradicate it.

Neither our original certainty nor these first accounts of the soul—as first principle of vital activities, as substantial form of an organized body—make any claims at all about what we may call the spirituality of the soul.

That the soul is immaterial follows from the fact that it is a form, and in that sense all substantial forms are immaterial—are forms, that is, and not matter. It is all but impossible to think of the human soul without being reminded of philosophical—think especially of Plato—and religious doctrines which hold that our soul preexisted its union with body or will survive death or both. Nothing like this is being claimed or assumed at the outset. That inner experience of life is not the experience of a spiritual thing, that is, of a thing that can exist apart from the body. What one is aware of is vital activities and that there is within us a capacity to perform them. If any of those activities or the soul itself turn out to be drastically different from other natural activities or substantial forms, that will have to be established by argument. It is not, again, the assumption of the discussion. At this point, materialists and nonmaterialists are one big happy family.

TEXT OF THE MASTER

Defining the Soul

[213]   Note that, as the Philosopher teaches in *Metaphysics* VII, there is this difference between the definition of substance and accident, that nothing is put into the definition of substance that is outside the substance being defined, since a substance is defined by its material and formal principles. But in the definition of an accident is put something outside the essence of the defined, namely, its subject: the accident's subject must enter into its definition. E.g., when we say "snubness is the curvature of the nose." The reason for this is that the definition signifies what a thing is: but substance is something complete in its existence and kind, whereas accident does not have complete existence, but is dependent on substance. Similarly no form is something complete in kind: that completeness of kind belongs to the composed substance. Therefore the composed substance is so defined that nothing outside its essence enters into the definition. But in the definition of form, something outside the essence of form is mentioned, namely, its proper subject or its matter. Hence, since soul is a form, it is necessary that its subject or matter enter into its definition.

[214]   So in the first place, he sets down two divisions, the first of which is necessary for investigating what is put into the definition of soul to express its essence, the second, what is necessary to investigate what is put in the definition of soul to express its subject, there, "Substantiae autem maxime, etc." In pursuit of the first he sets down three divisions, of which the first is that according to which being is divided into the ten categories. This he implies when he says that substance is one kind of being.

[215]   A second division is according as substance is divided into matter and form and composite. Matter indeed is

that which in itself is not a definite thing (*hoc aliquid*). Form
is that thanks to which the thing is now actual. The composed substance is a definite thing. That is called a definite
thing (*hoc aliquid*) which can be pointed out as complete in
being and kind and, among material things, this is true only
of the composed substance. For separate substances, though
not composed of matter and form, are definite things since
they actually subsist and are complete in their nature. The
rational soul can be called a definite thing in a way, insofar
as it can subsist by itself. But because it is not a complete species but is rather part of a species it cannot be said in every
way to be a definite thing. The difference between matter and
form is this: that matter is potential being, and form is entelechy, that is the act whereby the matter comes to be actually, such that the composite being actually is.

[216]   A third division is of two ways of understanding
act, the first as science is an act, the second as considering
is an act. The difference between these kinds of acts can be
seen from their correlative potencies. One can be called a potential grammarian before he acquires the skill of grammar
by discovery and being taught, the potency being actualized
when the habit of the science is had. But then he is in further
potency with respect to its use when he is not actually considering it. This potency is actualized when he actually uses
grammar. Thus both knowledge and its use can be called acts.

[217]   He sets down divisions needed to look into what
is put into the definition of soul as pertaining to its subject.
And he suggests three divisions, the first of which is a distinction between substances which are bodies and those which
are not. Bodily substances are the most obvious kind since
incorporeal substances, whatever they might be, are not manifest to us, as not falling within the range of sensation but in-
vestigable by reason alone. That is why he says "bodies especially seem to be substances."

[218]   A second division is between natural or physical
bodies and artificial bodies. Man and wood and stone are natural bodies, whereas house and hatchet are artificial. Natural

bodies seem more obviously substances than artificial ones because natural bodies are the principles of artificial bodies. Art works on matter provided by nature and the form imposed by art is an accidental form, just as shape and the like are. Thus, artificial bodies are not in the genus of substance because of their form but only because of their matter, which is natural. Their status as substance derives from natural bodies. That is why natural bodies are substances more than artificial bodies are because they are substances not only because of their matter but also because of their form.

[219]   A third division is between natural bodies which have life and those which do not. That is said to have life which by itself has nutriment, growth, and decrease. This is by way of illustration rather than definition since a thing is said to have life not only because of nutriment, growth, and decrease, but also because it senses and understands and can exercise other works of life. Hence in separate substances there is life because they have intellect and will, as is said in *Metaphysics* XII, though there is no growth or taking food with them. But because in generable and corruptible things the soul which is in plants, to which nutriment and growth pertain, is the beginning of life, and that is why by way of example he explains "having life" by nutriment and growth. The proper understanding of life is that something is capable of moving itself, taking move in a wide sense such that even intellectual activity can be called motion. We say things which are moved only by an external principle are without life.

[220]   He looks into the definition of soul on the basis of the foregoing distinctions. He does three things. First, he looks into the parts of the definition; second, he gives the definition; third, he responds to a difficulty. The first point is subdivided into two: first he examines the parts of the definition pertaining to the essence of the soul, second those which pertain to the essence of its subject. The first is further subdivided, for first he looks into this part, that the soul is an act, and then that it is first act.

From the foregoing, then, he concludes that, since physical

bodies are especially substances, and every body having life is a physical body, it must be said that every body having life is a substance. And since it is an actual being, it is necessary that it be a composed substance. Because when I say 'a body having life,' I say two things, namely that it is a body and a body of a certain kind, one having life. It could not be said that the part of the body having life which is called body is the soul. For by soul we mean that whereby the thing having life lives; so it must be understood as existing in a subject, taking subject here in a broad sense according to which not only what actually exists is called a subject, as an accident is said to be in a subject, but prime matter too is called a subject. The body which receives life is rather the subject or matter than what exists in a subject.

[221]   Thus since substance is threefold, namely, the composite, matter and form, and soul is not the composite 'body having life' nor the matter, that is, the body which is the subject of life, it remains that soul is a substance as the form or species of such a body, namely, of a physical body having life in potency.

Commentary on the De Anima, Book Two, lesson 1

14. BEYOND THE GRAVE

IN HIS youth, Aristotle wrote with a kind of Platonic insouciance of a future life when the soul would be freed from the body and soar off to its appropriate sphere. With age came the realization that such claims are anything but self-evident. So too Thomas, as Christian believer, lives in the expectation of a life beyond this one where complete fulfillment can be had. But Thomas no more than Aristotle regards as self-evident the claim that the human soul can enjoy a separate existence. How could such a thing be shown to be true?

Capacities for Vital Acts

In speaking of the life-world, we inevitably refer to our own experience of life and eventually we come to see ourselves as a kind of summing up of the cosmos. A microcosmos, as the medievals liked to say. That man exhibits activities of a peculiar kind is true enough, but it is also true that all types of activities are found in him. He falls like a rock, but he also grows like a plant and senses like an animal.

The fact that we are a natural or physical thing among other natural things makes applicable to us that initial analysis of change and the features of what has come to be as the result of change. Like everything else, we are made up of matter and form. It is when we move off from this initial, extremely abstract level and analyze the kinds and species beneath its vast umbrella that we take note of the difference between living and nonliving substances.

Our own experience of life gets into the first account we

123

give of the soul: that whereby we primarily live, grow, sense, remember, dream, desire, and think. The soul is known from the activities of which it is the source and, because it must be the primary source — living substances are not merely accidentally such — the next account of soul, as the substantial form of a physically organized body potentially having life, has in the life-world an application as broad as matter-form has in the natural world.

If soul is known, not by direct intuition, but by way of vital activities — seeing, hearing, hoping, etc. — the soul being that in us which enables us to do such things, we nonetheless cannot identify the soul as such with any one of these capacities. The reason is obvious enough. We begin with the barefoot belief that hearing is one thing and seeing is another. The capacity to hear cannot be identical with the capacity to see. If they were, the initial distinction between them would be threatened.

What does happen, can happen. What actually occurs relates to potentiality. To be actual and to be potential are correlatives. Actual seeing relates to potential seeing, actual hearing to potential hearing. If the activities are different, the power to perform them must differ. And such powers or capacities or faculties must be distinguished from the soul itself. If this were not done, the capacity to see would be one with the capacity to hear and that would entail that seeing and hearing are identical. But if we know anything, we know seeing is not identical with hearing. So the soul must be distinguished from its powers and their acts.

Aside

Notice how oblique and indirect Thomas's talk of the soul is (talk he learned from Aristotle). There is no suggestion at all of taking a look inside and seeing the soul and that it is not identical with its powers and activities. That kind of introspection is worse than a parody of Aristotelian procedure.

We begin with vital activities—seeing, hearing, moving our hand, breathing out and breathing in—that we are conscious of performing.

That they differ from one another is as certain as that they occur. It is when we observe that not everything in the physical universe exhibits these activities, that the distinction between the living and nonliving is made. The soul is introduced as the name for the peculiar kind of substantial form living substances have. The distinction of these activities from one another grounds the distinction of the powers from one another and mandates the distinction between the soul and its powers.

None of this relies on any special experience, none of it requires three credits in anything, none of it is "philosophical" or sophisticated. It is ordinary talk about ordinary certitudes. The initial analysis of these matters appeals to standards and principles of discussion everybody already possesses.

Layers of Life

Not only is there a variety of vital activities, they are ranked in terms of higher and lower. This may disturb your democratic impulses, but listen to the basis for the ranking.

Some vital activities are found in anything alive, some are found in fewer, and some are found only in man. The basis for the hierarchical arrangement is thus first of all how widely shared the activities are. Your worst fears of elitism are realized. What's wrong, I imagine you protesting, with being common and widely shared? And what's so special about being special? Man is the only species that starts forest fires but we don't pin a medal on him for that. There's another basis as well. Some vital acts are more distant from the kinds of activities any physical object can engage in, living or not, and that is the basis for saying they are more perfect. The more distant from purely natural activities, the more perfect vital activity is.

Sense Perception

The activities of the senses are analyzed on the model of change or becoming. We come to see such-and-such, we come to hear this-or-that. Just as Aristotle and Thomas argued from an analogy with accidental change to establish that the subject of substantial change had to be a non-substance (prime matter), so an analogy is established between physical change and coming to sense.

On the basis of this analogy, actual seeing is spoken of as the acquiring of a form, since all change results in a subject's having a new form. What is the subject of the change? The power of seeing. The eye? Not quite.

When I feel something, a physical change occurs in my body. If I touch something cold, my hand cools; if I touch something hot, my hand undergoes a physical change. While sensing is inconceivable apart from such changes, such changes are not what we mean by sensing. Why not? Because we do not say the poker with which we stir the fire feels the heat. We do not say the pot feels the soup. And so forth. But built into the account of sensation must be such physical changes. The hand acquires a new temperature, a new form. That is needed for touch but not equivalent to it.

Sensing is the reception of a form which does not result in a new instance of that form. The inventory of warm things is not increased when I perceive warmth, even though the changed temperature of my hand does add to that inventory. Paint a fence red and there is one more red thing in the world. Look at the red fence. Actually seeing it is a change from only potentially seeing it. Say that seeing is the reception of a form, red—but there is not another instance of red in the world because of that.

The reception of a form in perception differs from the reception of a form in matter. When a form is received in matter there is a new instance of that form. When a form is received in perception, there is not a new instance of that form.

The form in perception is not received as form is received in matter.

This is the origin of talk of immateriality. That talk accelerates when we turn to the activity of mind.

Thinking of Things

However different the reception of form is in sense perception, sensation is well below thinking. It is in thinking that we have the reception of a form, thanks to which a group of things are the kind of things they are, that does not intrinsically involve the kind of physical change sensation does, when the physical organ of sense has to undergo a physical change.

The basic analogy with physical change is kept. Coming to know things is as a kind of becoming the reception of a form. The intellect is the subject of the change, the form is what makes a range of things be the kind of things they are. Because the physical change of an organ is not intrinsically involved, thinking is further removed from the physical change whereby new individuals of a species come into being. The form received by mind does not make the mind another instance of that form, as if thinking of what makes rhinoceroses to be rhinoceroses altered the thinker literally into a beast of that sort.

Mind more than sense is a subject of a kind of becoming in which a form is received in a way different from the way form is received in matter.

That is what is meant by speaking of mental activity as immaterial. Such talk emerges in a straightforward way from analyzing what everybody already knows. It does not rely on some introspective intuition whereby we surprise a spiritual realm within ourselves. To speak of the immateriality of thinking is simply to say that our grasp of that which makes things to be a given sort does not produce another instance of that sort. That is to say a lot, of course, but it is not a matter of slipping in the immaterial when nobody is looking.

The Remedy of Thinking

Because physical change results in singular and individual things—this substance, this tan lady, that relocated pitchfork—the coming into being of one thing is the ceasing to be of another. Paleness has to go if I am to become tan; I can't be where I was if I am now here; the penalty of dieting is that I am no longer a pudgy 178. Unless the seed die, the plant cannot live.

In the physical world, things interact; there are causes and effects, indeed mutual causality is the mark of the physical realm. Things are ordered. But every thing is itself and not another thing, as Bishop Butler said. On several occasions, St. Thomas speaks of knowledge as a kind of remedy for the isolation of thing from thing. It is a way of being acted on which does not physically alter the recipient.

When I eat an apple, I have it in some sense, but of course the apple ceases to be. This does not happen when I look at the apple or smell it. Nor does it happen when I think of what it is that makes apples to be apples. To have the form of things in knowledge differs from having that form physically. We can have only one substantial form physically, but we can in principle know every kind of form there is. Thanks to knowledge, the whole universe can be writ small within our minds. Knowledge enables man to be a microcosm in a far more profound way.

Immortality

Aristotle and Thomas pin their philosophical arguments that the human soul can exist independently of the body after death on the character of thinking. The nature of thinking lifts the human soul, although it is the substantial form of a living body, free from the confining and restricting consequences of matter.

It is not uncommon to think that a human person cannot simply fade into dust because of the character of those activities which mark off humans from other natural entities. To have the capacity to think of galaxies and billions of years, to range over human history and the duration of our solar system, all this while sitting down, does not strike us as something that can be turned off like a light.

That hunch, if we have it, is what Aristotle and Thomas elaborate in their proof of the immortality of the human soul.

The upshot of that proof is for Aristotle puzzling and for Thomas dissatisfying. Aristotle almost never in his mature years talks about the soul after death. When he does, in the *Nicomachean Ethics*, the discussion seems fuzzy. The Christian belief in the resurrection of the body provides Thomas with a far richer conception of man's ultimate condition.

The nerve of the proof for the survivability of the soul is this. Thinking is an activity which does not intrinsically involve a bodily organ, and this provides the basis for saying that the soul whose power the mind is itself is capable of existing without matter.

TEXTS OF THE MASTER

Powers or Faculties of the Soul

I reply that it must be said that potency as potency is ordered to act so that a potency must be understood in terms of the act to which it is ordered and there will be a plurality of potencies insofar as there are diverse acts. Acts in turn are distinguished in terms of their objects. Every action is of either a passive or active potency and the object of a passive potency relates to its act as an efficient principle or cause: insofar as color moves sight it is the principle of seeing. The object of an active power relates to it as term and end: as the capacity of growth relates to an ideal size which is its goal. Action is the kind it is because of these, whether as principle or as end and term. . . . Potencies then are distinguished by their acts and objects.

The Remedy of Knowledge

Notice therefore that a thing is found to be perfected in two ways. First, according to the perfection of its existence, which belongs to it because of its proper species. But because the specific being of one thing is distinct from the specific being of another, therefore in any created thing having perfection of this kind there is lacking that much of absolute perfection as is found more perfectly in other species, such that the perfection anything has in itself is imperfect insofar as it is only a part of the total perfection of the universe which is arrived at by adding up the perfections scattered among things. Hence, that there might be some remedy for this imperfection there is found another manner of perfection in created things, insofar as the perfection proper to another thing is found in it, and this is the perfection of the knower as knower. Insofar as something is known by a knower it exists in a certain manner within the knower, which is why in *On the Soul* Aristotle said that the soul is in a way all things because it is capable of knowing them all. In this way it is possible for the perfection of the whole universe to exist in one thing. Hence this is the ultimate perfection the soul can achieve, philosophers say, that in it the whole order of the universe, and its causes, be inscribed, and they assign this as man's ultimate end which according to us will consist in the vision of God since, as Gregory put it, "what will they not see who see the one who sees all?" The perfection of one thing cannot be in another in the determinate existence it has in the thing itself, so in order for it to be in another it must be considered without that which makes it determinate. And since the forms and perfections of things are determined by matter, something will be knowable to the degree that it is separated from matter, which is why that in which this perfection is thus received must itself be immaterial. For if it were material, the received perfection would be in it according to a determined mode of existence and would thus not be in it as knowable, namely, insofar as, being the perfection of one thing, it is capable of being in another. . . . Thus Averroes says in commenting on the *De anima* that the form is not received in the possible intellect in the same way as it is received in prime matter; it is necessary that what is received in the knowing intellect be immaterial, and thus we see that according to the degrees of immateriality in things are there degrees of knowledge. Plants and the things below them can receive nothing immaterially and are wholly lacking in cognition. . . . The sense receives a species without matter yet with material conditions whereas the intellect receives them purified of material conditions. So too there is an order in knowable things. Material things, as Averroes says, are not intelligible unless we make them so, for they are intelligible in potency alone, but they are made actually intelligible by the light of the agent intellect, as colors becomes actually visible in the light of the sun.

Immaterial things are intelligible in themselves, hence are of themselves more knowable, although less knowable to us. Therefore since God is the end of separation from matter, since he is completely free of all potentiality, he is both the highest knower and the most knowable reality.

Disputed Question on Truth, Question 2, article 2.

15. METAPHOR AND ANALOGY

THE CONSTANT reader of Thomas Aquinas is amazed at the mileage the saint gets out of a minimal vocabulary. Certain words are used over and over again, in a variety of contexts, and it is not always easy to see why. Persistence leads to the conviction that there is method behind this parsimony. We talk about things insofar as we know them, Thomas likes to repeat, and the connections between the uses of the same term can thus reveal the order in which we came to know.

Variations on Form

We have a good instance of this if we reflect on the way in which the terms "form" and "matter" have been used, first as meaning, respectively, the shape of a thing and the material, particularly wood, that is shaped. These meanings are ready to hand from the work of the woodsman, the whittler, the birdhouse builder. These are products of human art, but we see that the artisan is reshaping the natural material and it is the smallest of steps to speak of the product of natural change as composed of matter and form.

In this use, the matter is no longer wood alone; it can be any natural thing or substance that undergoes change. Form is not merely external shape, but comes to mean such things as temperature and texture and color; it means the size and weight of a thing; it means its place. A thing thus has many forms. That is, a natural substance acquires a variety of characteristics as the result of various changes and we can say in

133

each case that it is a subject or matter that has acquired a new form.

These same terms were then extended to the elements of substantial change. Aristotle said·that prime matter is known by analogy. We set up a series of proportions, thus.

$\dfrac{\text{Shape}}{\text{Socrates}}$	$\dfrac{\text{Red}}{\text{Plato}}$	$\dfrac{\text{Here}}{\text{Thelma}}$	$\dfrac{\text{Heavy}}{\text{Fifi}}$	$\dfrac{\text{Human}}{\text{X}}$

The advantage of the procedure is this. Should you wonder what Thomas means by "form" in speaking of that which makes Socrates to be a man, you might be told that this is just some Aristotelian technical jargon he has picked up. This is libelous. Aristotelian prose is almost wholly free of jargon. It is what attracted Thomas to him. The correct assuagement of your wonderment is to say, "The use of 'form' to speak of what makes Socrates human puzzles, as it should. But think of the way in which we can distinguish things by their shapes. Here are some blocks. Some are round, some are square, some are triangles. You can see on the box that they were made by Ota Toy in Japan. By some process or other this shape was imposed on this plastic. The result of the process is shaped plastic, triangular shaped, square shaped, etc."

You may feel condescended to, but the art of teaching consists of tactful condescension. It is finding a point where the inquirer no longer wonders and proceeding from there back to what caused a problem. The very language of the tradition in which Thomas moves is meant to carry with it the history of its uses, not as an impediment, but as a precious illumination of the way in which later uses of the term grow out of earlier ones.

And the earlier ones bear on matters which are more easily known by human beings. If someone has trouble with the blocks, his trouble is more likely to be with English than with shapes. You discover he is a native speaker of Tagalog. Slipping into this crude but serviceable tongue, you swiftly establish contact with him.

The same terms are used to analyze coming to see and coming to know. In coming to see, the sense power as subject or matter acquires a new form; in coming to know, the intellect as subject or matter acquires a new form. There will be further extensions of these terms as well. For example, Thomas and Bonaventure will ask whether angels have matter as well as form.

Act and potency represent another set of correlatives that have a long and connected history in Aristotle and Thomas.

Metaphor

What if someone objects that this is merely making a fuss over metaphor. He will ask us to notice that the form received by mind when it comes to know has long been called a concept. This suggests that coming to know is like having a baby; it is a process of conception or conceiving which results in a child of the mind. Why not just call this, and the use of form and matter much touted above, metaphorical usage and go on to serious matters?

In a similar way, the form of the mind is called an idea. The etymology of this is from the verb 'to see'. The idea is what the mind sees. But what of the extension of 'see' from sense perception to a mental grasp? Is that a metaphor? When Conrad in his preface to *The Nigger of the Narcissus*, says that his task as a writer is above all to make us see, he is scarcely thinking of his uncanny ability to create an image. More than most writers, Conrad wants us to understand what it is to be a human agent.

So when we say, "I don't see it" when someone explains something to us in arithmetic, we are unlikely to mean either what we do with our eyes or with our imagination.

But what is the problem? We imagined someone dismissively describing what we are doing as a going on and on about mere metaphor. What is metaphor? (I will not insult you by repeating the mot, "If physics were all, what's a metaphor?") A metaphor is the use of the name of one thing to

speak of another. That is roughly Aristotle's definition in the
Poetics. Sometimes the thing spoken of metaphorically has a
name of its own. A variation on an Aristotelian example
would be this. A golfer whose ball has gone into the woods
sardonically asks his caddy for a number 9 axe. So too a
woodsman might ask his assistant for a nine iron when he
needs to clear away underbrush. The golf club is like the axe
in that it is the instrument of the golfer. The axe is like the
golf club, not because of the chips you can make with it, but
because it is the instrument of the woodsman. Aristotle sees
this kind of metaphor as based on an analogy or propor-
tionality.

$$\frac{\text{club}}{\text{golfer}} \qquad \frac{\text{axe}}{\text{woodsman}}$$

Metaphor results from the ability to see connections that might
be overlooked. A fresh metaphor surprises with its fittingness.
It tells us something. The metaphor is an essential element
in poetic discourse. It takes us from one thing to another in
such a way that the first casts light on the second.

If as the two of us watch Fifi walking rhythmically away
I murmur that Fifi is a centrifugal bumblepuppy you are unlikely to catch my meaning, assuming I have one. Metaphors
work only if the term extended is more known than the thing
it is extended to.

Why else are metaphors so concrete, sensual, palpable? They
put the matter before our eyes (another Aristotelian remark)
by using words whose meaning is some sensible thing. We
see it in the sense of imaging it, and then we see in a further
sense, see the connection, see the way the thing spoken of
metaphorically is illumined by being likened to something else.
A haughty demeanor is caught by the word 'supercilious' making raised eyebrows the sign of the inner attitude.

So the objector has put his finger on an important point.
Metaphors illumine, teach, connect. The etymology of 'metaphor' itself is to transfer, to transport. Moving trucks in Greece
have METAPHORA emblazoned on their sides. We carry a word

from the thing to which it belongs and lay it on another thing. 'Metaphor' is a metaphor.

Analogy

Some things spoken of metaphorically have names of their own. But sometimes this is not the case. A word whose meaning is already known is used to speak of something we come to know but which does not yet have a name. We could call it 'phlengo', of course, randomly taking any sound, but to do that would be to lose the route that took us to it. To do that would be to create a technical vocabulary, a jargon. If Aristotle had called the principle of life the phlengo, the made-up term would, of course, have no associations that could help us understand him. In fact, he chose psyche, breath, naming the soul from a sign and effect of its presence.

The limitation of metaphor is that it tells us what something is like, not what it is. Similes are overt metaphors, so to say, and when the poet plangently pleads that his love is like a red red rose we reel in emotional response. But what does it mean? All the nice things we associate with a freshly bloomed rose are somehow attached to Fifi LaRue. But what is she really like?

It is thanks to its meaning that a term is applied to a subject, and if the subject does not exhibit the meaning in a straightforward way we may nonetheless accept the remark, even marvel at its fittingness. Fifi is a rose. But we would scarcely say that 'rose' now has a new meaning according to which it can be applied to pretty girls. Look up 'rose' in the dictionary and you will not find pretty girl among the meanings listed. That is one way to see that a metaphor is involved. The term means something thanks to which it straightforwardly applies to A (this flower). When it is used of B (Fifi, of course), this is because of what we associate with things which are straightforwardly named by the term.

To be spoken of metaphorically is to share a term with other things but not to gain a direct and independent claim on the term in question. Is that what is going on when Aristotle and Thomas use 'form' and 'matter' in the way we recalled above? Is the form of the mind called a form only metaphorically? (We now know what 'only metaphorically' means.) Not necessarily. Metaphors sometimes prepare for another and more informative sharing of the same term.

"Things are said to be named equivocally when, though they share a comon name, the name means different things as used of each of them." That is the opening sentence in the *Works of Aristotle* as arranged by the Bekker in the ninteenth-century. When King Arthur cries, "Bring me my mail!" one servant brings him letters and another a suit of armor, thereby setting the table all aroar. Arthur's battle costume and his correspondence are both called 'mail'. They share the term. The term has one meaning as applied to armor, and another as applied to the post. In this case, it just happens that the same English word has these two meanings. There is no connection between the meanings. The term is equivocal. Both servants know English, they know the two meanings of 'mail', but one picked up the wrong signal in the context of the command. Arthur did not shout with the intention of being understood in both ways.

If a term is used equivocally when it has several meanings which are unrelated to one another, a term is used univocally when it is common to several things according to the same meaning. To speak of the armor of Arthur and of Prince Valiant as 'mail' is to use the term univocally. The same term has the same meaning in the two uses.

Metaphor is neither equivocation—the term used metaphorically does not have another meaning that explains the use—nor of course univocation. But there is another way in which a term can be shared which is like metaphor. Aristotle calls this controlled equivocation, Thomas calls it analogy. A term is used analogously when it has several meanings, one of which is primary and the focus of the others. Thomas regularly employs Aristotle's example of 'healthy'. I say that Fifi is healthy, that her complexion is healthy, that her diet is healthy. The common term here does not have one and the same meaning in all its uses, but neither are we likely to say that there is simply a plurality of unrelated meanings. Anything is denominated healthy from health. Fifi has health, her complexion is a sign of the health she has and her diet ensures that she will keep it. The focal meaning is 'having the quality health.' The other meanings presuppose and refer to this one.

It is this kind of controlled equivocation, an equivocation involving a focal meaning, or analogy that characterizes the language of the philosophical tradition in which Thomas moves. It is what controls his many uses of the same term, extending it in such a way that its meanings become a ladder on which we can mount from the easy and obvious to the difficult and obscure. This way of using terms—Thomas calls it analogous usage—is crucial in extending our knowledge beyond the physical to substances which exist without matter and ultimately to God.

A TEXT OF THE MASTER

On Naming God

I say that, as was pointed out, we know God from the perfections which come from Him to creatures, which perfections are indeed in God in a more eminent mode than they are in creatures. Our intellect, however, grasps them as they are in creatures and signifies them by words in the way they are grasped. That is why there are two things to be considered in names attributed to God, the perfections signified themselves — goodness, life, and the like — and the way of signifying them. With respect to what names of this kind signify, they belong properly to God, and more properly than to creatures and are said first of Him, but with respect to the mode of signifying they are not properly said of God, since they have a mode of signifying which is tied to creatures.

Some names signify such perfections which proceed from God to creatures in such a way that the imperfect way in which the creature participates in divine perfection is included in the very meaning of the word, as 'stone' signifies something existing materially; such names can only be said of God metaphorically. But some names signify the perfections absolutely without any mode of participating being included in their meaning, like 'being,' 'good,' and 'living' and such words are properly said of God.

Summa theologiae, First Part, Question 13, article 3

16. PROVING GOD EXISTS

THAT GOD exists is, for the believer, as plain as the nose on his face. From his mother's knee perhaps he has been taught to call on God, to praise and honor Him, to obey Him. Such talk blended with all the other things he learned as he learned his alphabet and colors and telephone number. The believer is no more likely to doubt the existence of God than of the world. Does this mean that he takes God to be as obvious as the world? Is God really as plain as the nose on his face?

A little reflection on the way he has been taught to think of God will show him this is not so. God has been spoken of as a father, as a judge, as a maker, as a shepherd and mother hen, as thunder and lightning, as a mighty fortress. God is always spoken of as like other things, the things He has made. He never seems to be described in terms proper to Himself.

St. Paul, in his Epistle to the Romans, begins by listing all the crimes and sins of the pagan Romans. This may seem unfair since pagans are not Christians, but Paul goes on. They are without excuse, he says, because they could come to know the invisible things of God from the things He has made. Reading this in her Bible, Fifi will believe it, believe it because it has been revealed. What is she believing? That revelation and faith are not necessary to come to knowledge of God and that to know God is to learn the human good and what we should do.

A curious thing. It is a matter of faith that faith is not absolutely necessary to achieve some knowledge of God. Thomas Aquinas no more than Fifi is in need of arguments for the existence of God. He already holds as true the proposition that God exists—on the basis of faith. But he like many before and after him was prompted by that passage in Paul to formulate proofs of the kind Paul seems to have in mind.

From this angle, we can see what a glorious thing Aristotle's philosophy was for Thomas. In Aristotle were to be found proofs for the existence of God which had been formulated by a man uninfluenced by revelation, Old Testament or New. There are proofs in Augustine, others in Anselm, but these were formulated by men for whom the issue was not in doubt. Aristotle loomed like a laboratory example. We can imagine the excitement with which Thomas pored over those passages in Aristotle where the pagan philosopher argues that the world of change and motion requires in order to be at all — and he thought it had always been — a first mover, itself unmoved. A Prime Mover.

The Structure of a Proof

Early in the twelfth century, Anselm of Canterbury — he was then Abbot of Bec in Normandy — formulated a proof that Thomas dismissed as little more than a trick. Anselm's proof continues to interest philosophers; indeed, it sometimes seems to be the only proof that interests philosophers. Anselm sought to show that once it got into your head that God is "that than which nothing greater can be thought," you could no longer reasonably deny that God existed.

One could go on and on about this effort (people do) but we are presenting the thought of Thomas Aquinas and he thought very little of Anselm's attempt. I mention it because it is so very different from the kinds of proof Thomas did think worked, several of which he found in Aristotle.

Anselm begins with the meaning of "God" and attempts to convince us that the denial of God's existence is incompatible with what "God" means. Now you might say that the meaning Anselm assigns to "God" invokes other things, indeed everything other than God, whatever is less than Him. But all that is involved is that God is greater and they are less. In terms of what? Thinkability. It is all very abstract.

Even if such a proof worked, Thomas would have thought it a bit of a hothouse item, something for experts. The first time we hear it, we have the feeling our leg is being pulled. What it lacks is any obvious attention to the way in which we know and the sorts of things we can lay claim to know.

A proof should move from what is known to what can come to be known on the basis of what is known. The conclusion is true because the premises are true, which is why, in analyzing the proof, in assessing it, we turn to the premises to see if they can bear the freight that is being put upon them. Anselm's proof is really a *reductio ad absurdum,* the kind of proof that is fitting when doubt is cast on the self-evident. But the existence of God is not self-evident to us, however familiar He may be.

The premises of a proof for the existence of God must be truths about the world. It is from the things that are made that we can come to knowledge of the invisible things of God. That is just what Aristotle's proof looks like. The world is such that the world cannot be all there is. If it is, and it is, there must be a cause of it quite unlike his effect. (I speak of the Prime Mover as a person because Aristotle did. One ruler is best, one ruler let there be.)

Why Does The World Need a Cause?

The world is an unwieldy place, it would seem, and one might doubt that we have an idea that matches the term. It seems synonymous with "everything" and what precisely does "everything" mean? If we said that everything has a cause, we would have to be ready to show that to be true of this thing and that thing and the other thing, on and on, through all the things that are. We could never establish the claim. Isn't a proof of the existence of God from the world going to run into the same difficulty?

Aristotle's proof of the Prime Mover comes at the end of

his *Physics*, a work in which, we remember, he was setting down truths of a high generality about whatever comes to be as the result of a change. He argued that any actuation of the potency of a subject requires an agent who is acting for an end. He also argued that while motion is the act of the moved thing and not of the mover as such, every physical mover is also, in a different respect, being moved by what it moves. Against that background he formulated an argument that can be stated briefly as follows.

Whatever is moved is moved by another.
There cannot be an infinite series of moved movers.
There must be a first unmoved mover.

It is unfair to the proof to make it look as if those three sentences in isolation are all it takes. The proof is dependent on everything that has preceded it in the *Physics*. But I provide it in the short form because that is what Thomas himself does. This is the first of the five ways of proving God exists that he sets down in a famous text. A glance at the premises will convince you that these are far from self-evident truths. They must in turn be proved.

The Nerve of the Proofs

It is the second premise that may seem most dubious to you, just on the face of it. If we think of a series of things such that *A* is caused by *B* and *B* by *C* and *C* by *D* and *D* by . . . Just keep going. Why not? If *A* can be explained by invoking *B*, and *B* by invoking *C*, you can just keep it up, going on forever, and everything will be explained without any need to bring in God, that is, a cause different from the ones that are already doing a good job. Remembering earlier remarks about the eternity of the world, you could add that this is just what Aristotle seems to assume. Eternity and infinity seem to remove the need for anything different from the things we start with.

This is a familiar kind of negative response to the proofs. The objector will say: if you want something eternal and unexplained, let it be the world, no need to bring in God. He may even in blasphemous exuberance allow that we can call the world 'God' if we need a use for the term.

What is puzzling is that it was precisely Aristotle who, though he held the world to be eternal, formulated the argument for a prime mover. Aristotle was not the village idiot, and we can assume his attention span was at least as great as ours. It wasn't that he forgot about claiming the world is eternal. That is an ingredient of the proof he is formulating. Chances are that the objector is missing something in Aristotle's effort. What could it be?

To explain *A* by *B* and *B* by *C* and *C* by *D*, and so on to infinity, does not explain why there are things of that kind. Given that there are such things, they can bring about other things like themselves, and carry on to a faretheewell, but Aristotle saw that if a thing could cause another thing of the same kind as itself, it could not be the cause of the kind of thing they both were. Why are there any things like that at all? To say that this one causes that one and that one another, does not address that question. That seems to be the reason why Aristotle, who thought the world had always been, did not think that a world containing only things that came to be as the result of a change could be all there was. There had to be at least one other cause, a cause of a different kind. An uncaused cause. God.

Some Other Puzzles

In a primer like this we can now pass blithely on. I need not repeat that this matter, like all the others discussed in our little handbook, needs much further elaboration. But we are introducing Thomas, not exhausting him.

Thomas did not think proofs of God's existence are easy. He noted that Aristotle maintained that they are the culminating concern of the philosopher, something possible only in wise and ripe old age. It is the rare bird who can formulate a sound proof of God's existence. It is much easier to formulate objections to them. We should not think that Thomas took St. Paul to be saying that it was the work of an afternoon to acquire conviction that God exists.

This provided him with the answer to one question that was bound to arise. Why does God reveal to us that He exists if we can come to know Him by using our minds? Because few would arrive at such knowledge and those who did would reach the goal late in life. But that God exists is of great moment for how we live our lives, early and late. So God in His mercy, revealed Himself to us.

Early on we mentioned the distinction Thomas makes in the things that have been revealed between the mysteries of faith (which can only be believed) and the preambles (which are in principle knowable). That God exists is the most basic preamble of faith. Thomas at first believed and then came to know that God can be known from the world; men can know He exists and some of His characteristics. This enabled Thomas to formulate the following argument.

The argument addresses another question Thomas put himself. Is it reasonable to give one's assent to truths he cannot understand? The mysteries of faith—the Trinity, the Incarnation and the like—cannot be known to be true in this life. Only on the basis of the gift of faith do we give our assent to these truths. Is this reasonable?

Here is the argument Thomas gives on behalf of an affirmative answer. If some of the things God has proposed for our belief can be known to be true, it is reasonable to accept the others as true. The preambles thus provide reasonable grounds for accepting the mysteries. Not that the mysteries are thereby proved to be true, of course. The argument is on behalf of the reasonableness of believing them.

TEXT OF THE MASTER

Can God's Existence Be Proved?

There are two kinds of demonstration, one by way of the cause, which is called *propter quid*, and this is from what is first simply speaking, another by way of effects which is called a *quia* demonstration, which is from what is first for us. For when an effect is more obvious to us than its cause, we proceed from the effect to knowledge of the cause. From any effect the existence of its proper cause can be demonstrated (if its effects are more obvious to us), since the effect depends on the cause, given the effect, the cause must exist. That God is, since this is not self-evident to us, is demonstrable through his known effects.

That God exists and other like things which can be known of God through natural reason, as is pointed out in Romans 1:19, are not articles of faith but preambles to the articles, for faith presupposes natural knowledge as grace presupposes nature and perfection the perfectable. Nothing prevents someone from accepting on faith what in itself is demonstrable and knowable if he does not understand the proof.

Summa theologiae, First Part, Question 2, article 2

17. SPEAKING OF GOD

THEOLOGY, WHETHER that in which philosophers engage or that based on Sacred Scripture, is talk about God. We have seen how the two of these differ, the former arising only from what anyone can know about the world and himself, the latter taking its rise from revelation. But they are as one in this: in speaking of God, they must apply to Him terms which have their natural habitat with creatures.

Anyone who goes to the Bible expecting to find a special terminology applying to God alone is in for a bit of a shock. God walks with Adam and Eve in the cool of the evening, he speaks to Moses from the burning bush, he admonishes, he cajoles, he repents of having made man. The imagery is rich and various. God is compared with animals meek and fierce, with natural phenomena. We look in vain for God to speak of Himself in terms appropriate to Him alone. He Who Is? Yes and no, as we shall see.

The mark of Thomas's vocabulary that we mentioned earlier—key words acquiring in an orderly way meanings which record the trajectory of the mind's journey—reaches its culmination in talk about God. Words with the humblest of origins will be stretched almost beyond recognition to convey something of the perfection and otherness of God.

Human knowledge begins in the senses. Words express what we know. Our language will, if only in its etymology, exhibit this anchor in the sensible, the easily and readily available. Words which first mean sensible things are extended to mean other things insofar as knowledge of them arises out of knowledge of the things first meant by those words.

The vocabulary of grammar and logic exhibit this trait.

The subject of a proposition is a foundation on which things are placed; genus derives from family and procreation; the copula has biological overtones; terms are like boundary stones and discourse is a stream which spreads out from a spring.

Our mathematical vocabulary owes much to the Arabic but such words as geometry invoke surveying as arithmetic does counting, numbering, and measuring the sensible. Our image of Einstein is of a man at a blackboard.

It does not matter to the point being made whether what is involved is etymology, metaphor, symbolism, or what Thomas calls analogy. They all reveal the primacy for us of the sensible, the palpable. It is the way of the human mind. And God, when He reveals Himself to us, mercifully makes use of our natural way of knowing even when He has in mind a supernatural goal. Is revelation really a concealment, then, God hidden behind the sensible?

If the sensible were opaque, this might be so. But sensible reality is a bridge to what is beyond sense. It is in reflecting on our knowledge of sensible things that we come to see that coming to know is very different from such things coming to be. The chalky squiggles on the board enable the mind to think of abstract entities. So, too, the world shows forth the glory of God.

Metaphorical Talk

If God were literally a fire, if he had a hand to place on Ezekiel exactly like a human hand, if he became angry as we do, if he literally stretched from end to end mightily, He would be a physical thing, something that has come to be, something caused and not the ultimate cause of all else. It is the rare believer indeed who understands such talk literally. The fervor with which we sing "He's got the whole world in His hand" does not entail a cosmic theory somewhat on the order of the turtle supporting the earth. Those words speak a truth. That's the way it is; it is like that. The image is rich in associations and they play upon our heart and imagination and lift them beyond the realm of the sensible.

That is the role of symbols and metaphors in Scripture. A symbol gathers together the sensible and more, the metaphor transfers a word from the sensible world and tries to put it down in the spiritual realm. The metaphorical use of a term does not involve a new meaning of the term, only a new reference. And the term metaphorically refers to something that is like that to which the term, thanks to its literal meaning, properly refers. A fire consumes and cleanses, the laying on of a hand is a bestowal of confidence and assigning of a task, one who is angry punishes, what spans the cosmos seems free of it, not an item in it.

Spelling out metaphors is a bit like explaining jokes, of course. Part of the power of metaphor is that it does not depend for its effect on our analyzing how it works. The shock of recognition is there, perhaps, but it is a confused recognition. Philosophy, alas, is a lot like explaining jokes, making the initially surprising and effective combination dull and, as it were, literal. No one laughs at an explained joke. The joke disappears with the explanation.

Analogous Talk

What Thomas calls analogy goes beyond metaphor by developing a new meaning for a term thanks to which it can refer to something its earlier meaning did not cover. As with metaphor, there is reference back to the first meaning but not in the same way. When we call Fifi's complexion healthy, we mean that it is a sign of her health, but "sign of health" is a new meaning of the term. Thomas will then say that "healthy" refers properly but not primarily to complexion. When we call Fifi's jogging healthy, we mean it will enable her to keep her health and "preservative of health" is a new though secondary meaning. "Subject of health" is the controlling or focal meaning of 'healthy'—Thomas calls it the primary analogate and it is present sotto voce in the other meanings.

After he has acknowledged that most of our talk about God is metaphorical and symbolical—as is most of God's talk when He reveals Himself to us—Thomas goes on to say that there are three general sorts of divine name, the negative, the relative, and the affirmative or positive. What does he mean?

When God is called Lord or creator, He is spoken of in a way that depends on other things, the things over which He is lord, the things He has created. 'Lord' and 'creator' are both relative in that sense. God is denominated from other things, and those other things are built right into the meaning of the name. If God is always named from creatures, need creatures enter into the meaning of the name?

When God is said to be infinite and eternal and simple we are being told what He is not rather than what He is. He is not composed, for then the composition would need a cause, He is not limited, He is not measured by time as are physical things. But what is He in himself?

The question may seem idle. If God can only be known and spoken of from creatures, to ask what He is in Himself may seem to demand an access to Him that is closed to us. What else can divine names be but relative and negative. Thomas holds that some are positive and analogous. They tell us, however imperfectly, what God is in Himself.

Thomas wants to be able to accommodate the sense we have that, however secondarily a name may be applied to God, He is what that name means in a far more perfect way than the creature whose name it first is. He is that father from whom all fatherhood is named, both in heaven and on earth.

We learn the meaning of 'father' from experience with our male parent. Later we learn the role our father played in our coming into being. We recognized that our physical existence is dependent on him as effect on cause, at least by way of origin. After a while we can survive by ourselves; we are fated by and large to outlive our parents. Whatever contingent and autobiographical associations the term may have for us, those with different backgrounds, even orphans, will agree that a father is a cause of the physical generation of offspring.

Our father in heaven is not our male parent. He does not have gender. We can understand calling him father in terms of many things we associate with male parents—indulgence, forgiveness, gifts we don't deserve, and the like—and these associations would ground the metaphorical use of the term. The term can become analogous in Thomas's sense if we leave out features essential to male parents and save what is in another way central to its meaning. A father is the cause of another's being. Put that way, our instinct is to say, but then God is far more of a father than any earthly parent. And so he is. He not only causes us to come into existence, but sustains us at every moment. He cannot cease to be, but if He did, we would be annihilated by that very fact.

Thomas recognizes a number of words which are used analogously of God. As such, they are extended to him from what they originally mean and name. He is only secondarily meant by them. But when we consider the core of these meanings, we say that, however it may be with our language and the trajectory of our knowledge, what is named last in these cases is the most perfect.

He Who Is

If God can be named analogously and thus properly, this is not to say that human language can encompass His reality. Our language is inherently defective for expressing what God is.

A swift way of seeing this is the following. God can be called wise and just analogously. There are meanings of both terms according to which they can properly be applied to God. But imperfectly. Is this merely a pious addendum? It has a quite definite meaning in Thomas. However properly God can be called wise, however true it is that He is the most perfect among wise beings, to call Him wise expresses His perfection in a partial way. A sign of this is that there is a plurality of analogous divine names. To call God just is to name him in a way that refers to his perfection in a partial way. To be wise is not the same thing as to be just.

Any attribute, any expression of the kind, God is X, catches the divine perfection by way of the meaning of X, a meaning whose origin is in created perfection. But there are many values for that variable, X, many divine names. It seems that every effort to express the divine perfection involves imperfection.

This is not at all the same situation as when Socrates is called wise and just and bald and Athenian and a war veteran. All these terms refer to him truly but there is a really different basis for the truth of each. Socrates is a complex, historical entity. But God is simple. In God there is no distinction between his wisdom and his justice.

The Book of Exodus suggested a term that seems to avoid these difficulties. God tells Moses that he can tell others that He Who Is has sent him. In reflecting on this, Thomas takes it to mean that God is, not in the sense of 'is wise' and 'is just' and 'is merciful', but is in the fullest sense of the term. That is, he is taking wise and just and merciful and the like to be restricting the range of 'is' so that 'God is wise' limits God's existence to what is expressed by the predicate.

If predicate adjectives restrict the copula, we can take the infinitive of the copula, to be, *esse*, existence, and say that God is unrestricted existence. This, Thomas concludes, is the least imperfect way of referring to God.

Adieu

This is the merest hint of what Thomas has to say about these matters. They are for him the most important matters, both as believer and as theologian. The theologian is one who speaks of God. Thomas's accounts of what is meant by calling God omnipotent and eternal and simple are not merely historical items. They enter into current discussions in philosophy of religion, sometimes even dominate those discussions, not as a voice from the past, but as a living companion in the quest for knowledge.

To say only this about Thomas's theology is a crime, but then this whole book is a felony. Let us turn now to Thomas's moral teaching.

TEXT OF THE MASTER

The Names of God

It is impossible that anything be predicated univocally of God and creatures. Any effect which is not even with the power of its cause receives a likeness of the agent but not of the same order but deficiently. That which exists divided and multiplied in the effects are in the cause simply and in the same way, as the sun with its one power produces diverse effects among lower things. In much the same way all the perfections of things, which are divided and multiplied in created things, exist unified in God. Thus when a name pertaining to a perfection is said of a creature, it signifies that perfection as definitionally distinct from others. For example, when a man is called wise, we mean a perfection distinct from the essence of man and from his potency and his existence and all like things. But when this word is said of God we do not mean to signify something distinct from his essence, power, or existence. Thus, when 'wise' is said of man it in a way circumscribes and comprehends the thing signified, but when it is said of God the thing signified is left uncomprehended, as exceeding the meaning of the name. Thus it is evident that 'wise' does not have the same meaning as said of God and creature. And so it is with other words. So nothing is said univocally of God and creature.

But neither are they said equivocally, as some maintain. If that were true, nothing could be known of God or demonstrated about Him but we would always be guilty of the fallacy of equivocation. Not only is this against the philosophers who demonstrated many things of God, but also against the Apostle who says "that the invisible things of God can be seen through knowledge of the things that are made" (Romans 1:19).

155

It ought to be said, therefore, that names of this kind are said of God and creatures according to analogy or proportion. This occurs in two ways, either because many have a proportion to one, as 'healthy' is said of medicine and urine insofar as each had an order and proportion to the health of the animal, the former causing it, the latter signifying it, or because the one has a proportion to the other, as 'healthy' is said of medicine and the animal, insofar as medicine is the cause of the health in the animal. That is the way some things are said analogically of God and creatures and not simply equivocally or univocally. We can only name God from creatures, as was said earlier. That is why whatever is said of creatures is said of them insofar as there is some order of creature to God as to its principle and cause in whom preexist all the perfections of things in an excellent manner. This kind of community is midway between pure equivocation and simple univocation. Nor in things said analogously is there one meaning, as with univocal terms, nor totally diverse meanings, as with equivocal terms. Rather the word is said in many ways insofar as it signifies different proportions to some one thing, as 'healthy' said of urine means the sign of the animal's health, and said of medicine means the cause of that same health.

Summa theologiae, First Part, Question 13, article 5

18. THE MEANING OF LIFE

THOMAS AQUINAS saw the meaning of life in the dramatic terms of his faith. By Original Sin the race has fallen from a primordial innocence and bliss. God promises a redeemer and at long last, in the fullness of time, Christ is born, true God and true man. His sacrifice is the redemption of mankind, making possible an eternal happiness with God. Christ is the way, the truth, and the life. An eternal happiness with God is our destiny. *La sua voluntad e nostra pace.*

This is the truth about the human situation. It tells us what the human good is. How then could Thomas possibly be interested in what pagan philosophers thought about the matter? Wouldn't their answers to the question, "What does it all mean?" inevitably be false?

This is no small question. If Plato and Aristotle ask what the human good is, what fulfills and perfects the human agent, in what does our happiness consist, and they say something different from the Christian—as they must—how can what they say fail to be false, if the Christian answer is the right one—as Thomas firmly believed?

There is another possibility. The philosophical answer may be inadequate but not false. If the right answer is such that we need revelation to know it, no pagan philosopher is going to come up with it. But if the right answer contains what the pagan philosopher says and more besides, the relation between the two is not that of true to false.

The parallel is this. Just as Thomas held that pagan philosophers arrived at some truths about God which are a small part of the package given in revelation, so too he thought they had come to knowledge of the human good which is an ele-

157

ment in the full picture given by Christian revelation. There are "preambles of faith" in the practical order too.

Natural Law

This was not just speculation on Thomas's part. As in the case of "preambles" in the usual sense, he is guided by St. Paul. The heathen has the law written in his heart, whether or not he hears the good news. Original Sin has weakened but not corrupted human nature. The main principles that should guide human conduct are naturally knowable by men. The theory that this is so is called Natural Law and we will say more of it later. For now, it is important to see that the theory can be seen as the basis for exchange between believer and non-believer on moral matters. There is a common base they share.

Remember Thomas asking why God would reveal things about Himself that men can in principle know on their own. His answer was that, however possible such knowledge may be, it is extremely hard to come by and much of a lifetime is needed to achieve solid truth in the area. Consider from this point of view the Ten Commandments.

The Decalogue given to Moses by God contains prohibitions of theft, lying, adultery, fornication, murder, impiety, and the like. Acts of this kind are not wrong because God says so, as if prior to the Tables of the Law it was all right for men to lie and steal and murder and rape, but suddenly, by fiat, they become wrong because forbidden. In other cultures, such actions were seen to be wrong without benefit of revelation. Why then did God bother? A people can breach the moral law so long and so thoroughly that they become confused about what it is. The Tables of the Law were meant to remedy that kind of situation.

It will occur to some to say that it is the influence of Christianity—the Judeo-Christian heritage—that explains why the prohibitions of the Decalogue show up in manmade law as well. But a murderer who defended himself by saying he rejected the Bible and with it the Ten Commandments would not be released as having been mistakenly arrested. The prohibition of murder is the law of the land.

Some law is made—by man, by God—but there is as well the natural law, also deriving from God, as nature itself does. We can come to know the major precepts of natural law by using our heads. And that is the most sweeping one—use your head. We must do good and avoid evil. We are held responsible for what we do because we knowingly do this rather than that. Why? Why is murder wrong? Because it is destructive of society and man is naturally a social animal whose good is a common and shared one. The beginning of an answer, but the point is not to develop it fully, but to indicate how we go about dealing with moral questions.

Ultimate End

All human activity is purposive, Aristotle says in the *Ethics*; whatever we put our minds to, whatever we consciously and freely do, is undertaken with an end or good in view. It may be some objective reached by means of what we do; it may be simply doing something well, like playing the sweet potato or ocarina. Why are you doing that? Just cuz. It's an end in itself, not an activity without purpose.

Whatever is sought in action as its end or goal is sought as a good, that is, as fullfilling or perfective of the agent. The good is what all things seek.

Where there are ends, we will often recognize means of achieving them. Sometimes means are desirable only because they bring about the end; in themselves they are repulsive, like bitter medicine, getting your teeth drilled, jogging. Sometimes something is desirable in itself, endlike, but also instrumental in bringing about another end. We can cluster actions. Taken singly, whatever we do is for the sake of an end, but those ends will be as various and numerous as the things we do. Clustering introduces a unity or order in various realms of action. A number of different activities, each having its own end, can be clustered and become the military arts, and then they are directed to a common good, victory and peace. So, too, a variety of medical arts cluster under the direction of the doctor who aims them all at health.

What if all the things we do could be brought together in that way and aimed at a great good which is the end of all the other ends? Such an ultimate end would be something we should know about. Acting with an eye to it would ensure that what we do is good.

Not many philosophers nowadays share Thomas's view that Aristotle satisfactorily established that there is such an overriding ultimate end of human life. If there is, it is of course the answer to "What does it all mean?" If we take a glance at some standard objections, we will be better able to appreciate Thomas's defense of the claim that there is an ultimate end at which each particular human action should aim.

Some Objections

Sometimes Aristotle is thought to have made a dumb logical mistake. From the claim that every action aims at some good he mistakenly concluded that there is some (one) good at which all actions aim. Granted there is fun in trying to catch the Father of Logic in a logical blunder, but the fact is Aristotle never argues in that way.

He notes that the ends of actions are many and various, but that some actions are clustered in such a way that the ends of some are subordinated to an overriding end. If there were an end to which all our other aims were subordinated this would be our chief good. That's what Aristotle means by the ultimate end. And, he goes on, there must be an ultimate end of human action.

Why? Aristotle's argument is found in parenthesis in the text. It has been established that one end can be desired for another. Either that process comes to an end which is sought for itself alone and not for the sake of anything else, and the point is made, or there is no such end. Then whatever end is sought is sought in turn for something further, and that further end for yet another, and so on without end. But this cannot be.

Thomas sees the proof Aristotle offers as a reductio ad absurdum. The structure of such a proof is:

$P.v. -P.$
But $-P$ is impossible.
Therefore $P.$

P = there is some best and chief end of all we do. $-P$ is its contradictory opposite. How can $-P$ be seen to be impossible?

> If it were the case that the pursuit of ends goes on infinitely, such that one end is always pursued for the sake of another and so on to infinity, it would never come about that man achieves his desired ends. But to desire and pursue what cannot be achieved is senseless and absurd, so the pursuit of ends is senseless and absurd. But the desire for the end is natural: the good is what all things naturally seek. So it follows that a natural desire is senseless and absurd. But that is impossible. A natural desire is nothing else than an inclination inherent in things by the ordering of the Prime Mover, who cannot be frustrated. Therefore it is impossible that there be a subordination of end to end to infinity. (In I Ethics, lect. 2, n. 21)

So the argument form is a reductio, not a fallacious turning about of a proposition. Not that it isn't open to endless discussion—well, not endless. What would be the point of that?

Another Argument

The argument just sketched is found in Thomas's commentary on Aristotle's *Ethics*. In the *Summa theologiae*, he formulates another argument. Is it the case that there is an ultimate end of all human acts? The term "ultimate end" means "the

ultimate perfection and fulfillment of the agent." This is the
reason anyone acts, so in that sense there is one ultimate end
recognized by all men. As to what is seen to constitute the
ultimate perfection and fulfillment of desire, on that men differ widely and there may seem to be a great many ultimate
ends.

This argument depends on what is meant by saying of an
action that it is good. The assumption is that no matter what
anyone does, he does it because he thinks it is a good thing
to do. What does it mean to say that it is good? There could
be a quite limited answer to that question, of course. Fifi wants
yogurt because it is good for her. Meaning it is conducive
to health. Health presumably is either the good or a compo-
nent of the good. The agent wants whatever she wants as conducive to fulfillment or perfection. This is what Thomas takes
ultimate end to mean and he argues that no one can fail to
act for it. At the same time, he allows for the disagreement
among men as to what our comprehensive good is.

Neither Thomas nor Aristotle holds the idiotic view that
every man and woman in the world would right now give
you the same answer to the question, "What is the ultimate
meaning of life, what is the human good?" Both men explicitly deny that any such happy state of affairs exists.

Both men maintain that it is part of the logic of human
action that whatever we do is done under the implicit assumption that it is well for us to act that way. We will be the better
for it. It will lead to our good. That notion of our good in
a comprehensive sense is what every man and woman right
now acts in the light of.

This is not unanimity as to what precisely the comprehensive good of human agents is. Some will deny that there is
even this formal unanimity, and interesting objections have
been raised. Some will allow the formal unanimity—it seems
an easy concession—but add that there is no single objective
that could fill the bill. Different folks have different ends.
Different ultimate objectives. There is irreducible variety. Fifi

wants to be the leading woman philosopher in Watertown, Arizona. Her father bent his every action to being the best undertaker in Tombstone. Her mother just wanted to be left alone so she could read Father Dowling mysteries. And so it goes.

Like Aristotle, Thomas thinks that in the nature of things there is a single substantive ultimate end for all human agents. But to hold that is by no means to deny the interesting differences between Fifi and her parents.

TEXT OF THE MASTER

Natural Law

Since law, as has been said, is a rule or measure, it can be in something in two ways, either as in the one ruling and measuring, or as in the ruled and measured. Something is ruled or measured to the degree that it participates something of the rule or measure. Thus since all things are subject to divine providence, they are ruled and measured by eternal law. It is obvious that all things participate in some way in eternal law insofar as from its influence they have inclinations to their proper acts and ends. The rational creature is subject to divine providence in a more excellent way than other things, insofar as he is made a participant in providence itself, providing for himself and others. Thanks to his participation in eternal law he has a natural inclination to his fitting act and end. The rational creature's participation in eternal law is called natural law. Hence, when the psalmist said, "Sacrifice the sacrifice of justice," it was as if answering those asking what the works of justice are that he added, "Many ask, 'Who will show us what is good?'" to which question he responds, "The light of thy countenance is sealed upon us, O Lord." As if the light of natural reason in which we discern what is good and what is evil, which pertain to natural law, is nothing other than the impression of the divine light in us. Thus it is clear that natural law is nothing other than the rational creature's participation in eternal law.

Summa theologiae, First Part of the Second Part, Question 91, article 2

19. ON BEING GOOD

FIFI'S APARTMENT is on the first floor and one morning she throws open the window, thrusts her head into the invigorating air, and is showered by a dishpan of suds from on high. The occupant of the apartment upstairs is abject. Fifi, lovely girl, laughs it off. "That's all right. No harm done."

Fateful remark. Her neighbor, debonair, good looking, weak chinned, is a philosopher. His expression of relief is replaced by one difficult to describe. The word 'smug' suggests itself.

"I couldn't agree more," he cries.

Fifi, toweling her just shampooed hair, is nonplussed. Her neighbor is all too willing to explain. His name is Legion. He is even now completing his doctoral dissertation.

"Do no harm to others. It is the only moral absolute."

He explains through much of the morning that he has proved beyond the shadow of a doubt that the history of moral philosophy is a record of bad arguments and unpersuasive exhortation. He proposes to cut through all the crap and begin and end with a single moral principle. Do no harm to others.

Among the many merits Legion sees in his proposal is that moral philosophers can get out of the business of assessing and appraising what people choose to do. Legion would leave them to their own devices. With one proviso. They must not harm one another.

"Why not?" Fifi asks, the question prompted perhaps by the murderous thoughts that have been assailing her during Legion's lengthy lecture.

"Would you want someone to harm you?"

"I want to harm someone else."

165

"Who may want to harm you."

Who already has, she thinks, though her pretty smile does not falter.

Legion lauds his own position as free of any assumptions about moral absolutes and human nature and things we ought to do just because of the way we are made. Or evolved. His smile is toothy and conspiratorial.

"Just think," he says at the door to which she eventually leads him. "If I hadn't done dishes this morning, we wouldn't have met."

"Yes," Fifi muses, mentally resolving to send him a year's supply of paper plates.

Fifi's Reflections

In the days that follow, Fifi, a thoughtful girl, thinks about these things. What Legion has said, but not Legion himself, interests her. Him she avoids. She slips in and out of the building; she adopts a thick foreign accent in answering the phone and chirps about orders of fried rice being on their way when she recognizes his voice.

Why, she wonders, would anyone think he had escaped a natural measure for moral judgments by settling on the notion of harm? Even if one took harm to be the only moral evil and avoiding it the only moral imperative, this is to get oneself in very deep indeed.

What is harm in this usage? Pain? That can't be. Dentists, dieticians, punishing parents, and exercise all inflict pain, but the pain is taken to be all right because it is for something else. Something good. Which is more than the absence of pain.

A dentist's disquisition on dental health is not put forward as subjective. "I think cavities are bad, but that's just my opinion. Some people like them. Why, there's an island in the Pacific. . . ." Dentists don't talk that way.

So too dieticians and physical therapists and parents have

an end in view when they attend to ours. The pain their ministrations involve leads on to a proper weight, a desirable agility, rectitude.

Pain is good or bad depending on whether or not it is harmful. And, it seems to Fifi, we think there are objective measures of what is or is not harmful to human beings. Our knowledge of health may be imperfect, but we know where to look to perfect it.

Legion may not like it, but Fifi sees his moral theory as a minimal version of natural law. Because harm must apply to more than health. To isolate someone from others is to do him harm. To prevent someone from learning is to do him harm. To prevent men and women from marrying and having children is to do them harm. Harm means thwarting the pursuit of what is fulfilling or good. Without an objective measure of goodness, harm makes no sense.

The more she thinks of it, Fifi sees a rich moral theory springing from Legion's notion of harm. It is a theory so rich it contains a justification for her continued avoidance of her upstairs neighbor.

Moral Commonplaces

The moral comes into play when we act consciously. Digesting lunch, blinking my eyes, breathing are things I do not consciously do. I do them in my sleep. I am unlikely to be asked why I am doing them. The relevance of Why is the sign that we are in the moral realm. The question assumes that we know what we are doing and are deliberately doing it.

Acting consciously involves taking into account things which are not what they are because of us. Like health. Like the fact that humans are born into societies and would not survive outside them. Like the fact that boys are attracted to girls and vice versa because the race will go on only if they mate and have children. Like the fact that we have a mind. Reflecting on such facts gives rise to judgments about what to do.

The most general judgments of that sort, the inescapable ones, make up what Thomas means by Natural Law.

I must put my mind to doing what is right and avoiding the opposite. This vastly general assumption is embedded in any conscious act. That my desire for food and drink is not a law unto itself, but should be governed by mind is inescapably true. To deny it is to accept it. Think about it. And so with sex. And social interactions. Human agents must put their minds to these in order to do them well. They can always be asked Why and they should have an answer.

So viewed, it turns out that it is difficult not to hold to what Thomas calls Natural Law. Not that it is often held under that name, but that doesn't matter. As Fifi has surmised, Legion, who thinks he is rejecting an objective basis for morality, is actually asserting it. And his position can scarcely be as lean as he thinks it is.

Natural Law consists of moral commonplaces. The theory is that these are the sweeping judgments anyone is going to make as a moral agent. If not explicitly formulated, they are embedded in the judgments that are formulated. Just as the Principle of Contradiction is seldom formulated outside philosophy courses but, once formulated is seen to be what one held all along, so too the starting points of moral reasoning will be found implicit in the moral outlook of mankind.

Less Common Judgments

As soon as we get away from moral commonplaces, things get murky as to what ought to be done. The answers are no longer unassailable. If true, they are true by and large, for the most part. But it is easy to imagine circumstances in which their point would be thwarted if we abided by them. Moral philosophy, ethics, the attempt to formulate somewhat less general advice is incorrigibly corrigible.

This is not to deny that there are many judgments that are by and large true and that survive the ravages of time.

But judgments about usury are made within the context of an economic system and will lose relevance if the system is replaced. Rules of justice will be contextual too and fairness has to be discussed in terms of particular social and political arrangements.

Even within a well-understood context, the question of what one ought to do cannot be decisively settled at the level of discussion. There are no ethical rules that just fit onto any old situation automatically. At the heart of morality is the agent who has to bring whatever previous explicit thinking he has engaged in to bear on these circumstances here and now. The knack of doing this, the virtue, is called prudence by St. Thomas, a good word that has fallen on bad times. For us the prudent person is a careful calculating one, looking out for Number One. Thomas has in mind the practically wise man who, desiring the good, with a past history of pursuit of the good, judges the here and now in the light of the good to which he is committed.

There is no neutral technique for generating particular moral judgments. To be able to judge well with regularity as to what ought to be done depends on one's heart being in the right place. In order to get a picture of what Thomas means by the prudent person, think of someone from whom you would solicit advice about a matter of moral moment.

Moral discourse has the moral commonplaces of Natural Law at one end and singular judgments in fleeting and unrepeatable circumstances at the other, and in between are general judgments which can guide us for the most part but it is up to us to judge when and how and where and how much. There are no rules for applying rules. For that we need prudence.

TEXT OF THE MASTER

Levels of Precept

The moral precepts, as opposed to the ceremonial and judicial, deal with those things which of themselves pertain to good mores. Since human mores are such with reference to reason, which is the proper principle of human acts, those mores are called good which are congruent with reason and those evil which are discordant with it. Just as every judgment of speculative reason proceeds from a natural knowledge of first principles, so every judgment of practical reason proceeds from naturally known principles, as was said earlier. From these, it goes on in different ways to judge of various things. (a) For there are some things in human acts so explicit that with the slightest consideration they can be approved or disapproved by means of common and first principles. (b) Some things are such that judgment about them requires much consideration of different circumstances—a diligent consideration which falls not to all but to the wise, no more than a diligent consideration of scientific conclusions falls to all, but rather to philosophers. (c) In order to judge some things, man needs divine instruction; e.g., things to be believed.

It is obvious, then, that since moral precepts concern the things that pertain to good mores, and these are in accord with reason, and every judgment of human reason derives in some way from natural reason, that all moral precepts necessarily pertain to the law of nature, but in different ways. (a) There are some things any mind judges right off ought to be done or not be done; for example, Honor your father and mother; Do not kill; Do not steal. Such judgments are absolutely of the law of nature. (b) Some things the wise, after a more subtle consideration of reason, judge ought to be observed. Such things are of the law of nature but require learning whereby the many are instructed by the wise. For example, "Stand up in the presence of a gray head and honor the person of the old." (Lev. 19:32) (c) Some things are such that human reason needs divine instruction, whereby we are instructed in divine things, if it is to judge them. For example, "Do not make for yourself a graven image nor any likeness" and "Do not take the name of God in vain."

Summa theologiae, First Part of the Second Part, Question 100, article 1

20. ARISTOTLE AND THE BEATIFIC VISION

SOMEWHERE IN a passage I can no longer find Chesterton wrote that the young man knocking on the brothel door is looking for God. It sticks in the mind. It surprises with its rightness. Every human agent is seeking the good, however mistakenly, but we all want what is really good. God is our real good. So no matter what we are doing we are seeking Him.

Implicitly, of course. The young man's query when the door is opened is scarcely theological.

The ultimate end is not sought instead of other ends; it can only be sought through them.

Let us end by returning to the matter of the relationship between philosophical and Christian morality.

The Supernatural

The Christian faith in the fall and redemption of man is not that Christ's sacrifice restored us to the condition lost by Original Sin. The good news is better than that. We are now, thanks to Christ's grace, called to a good that far exceeds our nature, one we could not dream of, let alone attain, save by his saving grace. Our last state is far better than it would have been if our first parents had not sinned. This is why Augustine was emboldened to call Original Sin a happy fault.

This destiny and the special means needed to achieve our new and gratuitous end is the basis of talk about the supernatural order. It does not refer to things above man, angels, say, but to a human capacity with the aid of grace to surpass what belongs to our nature. The supernatural order does not destroy the natural, but presupposes and builds upon it. Hence the prefix. It is this central teaching of Thomas that is the basis for exchange between believers and nonbelievers, between Christians and pagans, between Thomas and Aristotle.

For the Christian, the natural remains part of the package, though by and large believers don't sort out from what they think they ought do things that anyone, believer or not, ought to do. They will be more prompted to do this if they live in a society containing large numbers of nonbelievers. The sorting can easily be faulty, and it may be that Christians will lay on others obligations which only follow from accepting as true what Christ has taught. Non-Christians, however, in attempting to lay out a "natural ethics" will make mistakes of a parallel kind, unwittingly including precepts only a Christian is likely to acknowledge.

What could be better than to have the effort of a pagan to lay out what the human good is and what is needed to attain it? Thomas did not have to imagine what an ethics apart from religious belief would look like. He could read the *Nicomachean Ethics* of Aristotle. And he did. He even wrote an interlinear commentary on it, probably at the same time he was writing the moral part of the *Summa theologiae*.

How does what Aristotle said about the ultimate end of human striving compare with what Thomas said about the same subject?

Imperfect Felicity

After his conversion, Graham Greene wrote several essays on Henry James in which he discovers hitherto overlooked interests of the Master in religious matters. What he finds is really there but it is doubtful that a reader lacking Greene's suddenly sensitive antennae would have picked them up. There is something similar in Thomas's noting that Aristotle admits the happiness he sketches falls short of the notion of happiness.

> What is to come is unclear to us, and we hold that felicity is an end in every way complete. If this is so, we shall call happy those among the living who are and will be as described—but happy as men are happy. (1101a17–21)

Happy as men are happy. That is what Thomas seizes upon as a recognition by Aristotle that the felicity achievable by living men is imperfect. For one thing, it can be lost. It is subject to forces over which we have no control. Aristotle has set down the characteristics of happiness and they can only be imperfectly achieved in this life.

That is what the text says, as any reader can see, but it took a Thomas to find there the recognition by Aristotle that whatever happiness we achieve in this life falls short of the ideal. Our perfection or fulfillment, insofar as we can attain it, is imperfect, unfulfilled.

Why is this important? Because the believer's claim that the natural happiness Aristotle speaks of is only part of a larger package was in some implicit way recognized by the great pagan philosopher himself.

This is not, of course, to say that Aristotle had an intimation of the beatific vision and thereby had a measure according to which what he was describing as happiness fell short. When Aristotle defined happiness as a state that is final and self-sufficient and cannot be lost when gained, he was spelling out what he took to be implicit in all human striving. It is as if the logic of our actions reveals that our acts cannot perfectly achieve their aim. That is all. It is from Thomas's perspective that this passage takes on a deeper significance.

How Many Ultimate Ends?

By now you may wonder what is going on. An ultimate end, one would think, is last and final, the end of the chain, that after which nothing more is needed. But haven't I been suggesting that for Thomas there is another end beyond the ultimate end of Aristotle? Has Aristotle's ultimate end now become a penultimate end?

Remember Thomas's distinction between the definition of ultimate end, on the one hand, and what saves that definition on the other. The first is formal: the complete and fulfilling good which is sought at least implicitly in any particular action with its quite particular end or good. As to what actually fills the bill, there is disagreement among men. Some think the ultimate point of action is power, others pleasure, others wealth. The assumption is that they are agreed on the definition of ultimate end but differ on what saves the definition.

Presumably Aristotle wants to argue on behalf of what truly does save the definition of ultimate end. He does. It is an activity of soul in accord with perfect virtue. It is useful to know how he arrived at that.

If we ask when a man is a good man, the question is like asking when a car is a good car or a knife is a good knife or even when a golfer is a good golfer. A car is a good one if it fulfills its function, so is a knife and a golfer. It is when you know what something is for that you have a basis for saying whether or not it is a good one.

Now if man is for something, if he has what Aristotle calls a function, we will have a basis for saying when a man is a good man. How go about identifying the human function? Well, when we ask if the knife is a good one, we ask how it cuts, not whether it is a good paperweight. In other words, we ask about the knife as a knife. What is said of man as man? What is the specifically human activity?

There are some activities which are true of men, but not as men; they aren't peculiar to human beings. Fifi grows and digests, but so do plants and animals. She sees and hears, but beasts do that. To hear well is a good thing but not a basis for saying someone is a good person. It is reason that is peculiar to man, that is the activity that belongs to man as a man, and not to man as a thing or as a plant or an animal. So we are home free. To perform his distinctive activity well will make a man a good man.

The term 'virtue' is used to express the good performance of an activity. To do something well is to do it virtuously. The human good then is to act rationally well.

The function of a knife may seem simple enough, particularly if we specify carving knife or hunting knife or fish knife, but man's function is as complicated as that of the Swiss Army knife. Rational activity can mean the activity of reason itself, or other acts insofar as they come under the control of reason. It turns out that the phrase covers an ordered set, and the human good thus consists of a plurality of virtues. Hierarchically arranged. Aristotle teaches that contemplation, performing well the highest activity of theoretical reasoning, is the virtue for the sake of which all the other virtues should be sought.

Another short form of a long story, but it gives us some sense of how Aristotle speaks of what it is that saves the notion of ultimate end. And it is this, Thomas says, that Aristotle himself recognizes as fulfilling the definition only imperfectly. But it is the kind of happiness attainable by living men.

If this is imperfect happiness, what is perfect happiness? Union with God in the next life, a happiness which is complete and can never be lost once had. This is man's ultimate end, the beatific vision.

So: is Aristotle's ultimate end less than the ultimate end? Yes and no. It does not express what we are now called to, but how could it? Aristotle would have needed revelation to know that we are destined for a perfect happiness beyond this life. But what he has defined is ultimate this side of the grave for natural man.

This must be qualified, however, since it is possible to begin eternal life in this one. But as Aristotle said of the happiness of the living, as long as one is alive he can lose the state of grace. In this life, happiness is imperfect.

Once again, the upshot of Thomas's effort is to find a complementarity between philosophy and the faith. Not just any philosophy. His predilection is for the philosophy of Aristotle, though as we mentioned earlier his interest did not stop there.

St. Thomas was not, of course, surprised that there should be no conflict between reason and faith, but he marveled at the achievements of Aristotelian philosophy. He himself was primarily a theologian but he knew who *the* philosopher was.

TEXT OF THE MASTER

Is Happiness Achievable?

Can man acquire happiness through his natural powers? I answer that the imperfect happiness which can be had in this life can be acquired by man through his natural powers, in the same way that virtue can, in whose activity such happiness consists. But the perfect happiness of man consists in the vision of the divine essence. To see God in His essence is not only beyond human nature but beyond all creatures, as we showed in Part One. The natural knowledge of any creature is according to the manner of its substance, as the *Book of Causes* says of Intelligence, "that it knows both what is above it and what is below it according to the mode of its substance." Any knowledge which is according to the mode of created substance falls short of vision of the divine essence, which infinitely exceeds all created substance. Hence neither man nor any other creature can achieve ultimate happiness through its own powers.

Summa theologiae, First Part of Second Part, Question 5, article 5

Do All Men Desire Happiness?

Happiness can be understood in two ways. First, according to the common understanding of happiness, and in this sense it is necessary that every man desire happiness. The common understanding of happiness is that it is the perfect good. Since good is the object of will, the perfect good of anything is that which completely satisfies its will. Hence to desire happiness is nothing other than wanting one's will to be satisfied. Which anybody wants.

Second, we can speak of happiness in a special understanding, with respect to that in which happiness consists. But so considered not everyone knows happiness because they do not know what fits the common understanding. Consequently, in this respect, not all will it.

Summa theologiae, First Part of Second Part, Question 5, article 8

BIBLIOGRAPHICAL NOTES

1. Getting into Philosophy

Karl Jaspers, Bertrand Russell, A. J. Ayer, and a surprising number of the most important philosophers of our time have written introductory works. The recent book by Thomas Nagel, *What Does It All Mean?* (New York: Oxford University Press, 1987) is an excellent example of an outlook diametrically opposed to the Thomistic. Many of the great Thomists of our time have written introductions to philosophy. Jacques Maritain's *Introduction to Philosophy*, reprint (Westminster, Md.: Christian Classics, 1989), lacks his usual flair, but is solid and worthwhile. Etienne Gilson's *God and Philosophy* (New Haven, Conn.: Yale University Press, 1941) and his polemical work, *Being and Some Philosophers* (Toronto: Pontifical Institute of Mediaeval Studies [PIMS], 1952) provide good examples of the Thomistic mind at work. My own *St. Thomas Aquinas* (Notre Dame, Ind.: University of Notre Dame Press, 1982) has been found useful, but there can be no substitute for Josef Pieper's *The Silence of St. Thomas* (New York: Pantheon, 1957) and his *Scholasticism* (New York: Pantheon, 1960). On the question of the Church's interest in where we begin philosophy, see my *Thomism in an Age of Renewal* (Notre Dame, Ind.: University of Notre Dame Press, 1968). Many of the essays in Mortimer Adler's *Reforming Education: The Opening of the American Mind*, edited by Geraldine van Doren (New York: Macmillan, 1988) are pertinent to the themes of this chapter. See Josef Pieper, *Leisure, the Basis of Culture*, with an introduction by T. S. Eliot (New York: Pantheon, 1952).

2. Philosophy vs Religion

See the texts in Mary Clark's *Aquinas Reader* (New York: Fordham University Press, 1988), pp. 404–411, and my *St. Thomas Aquinas*, pp. 140–145. Josef Pieper's *Belief and Faith* (New York: Pantheon, 1963) is good on St. Thomas but also discusses Newman and the Jaspers of *Philosophical Faith*. Jacques Maritain, *The Angelic Doctor* (New York: Meridian, 1959). Vernon Bourke, *Aquinas* (Milwaukee, Wisc.: Bruce Publishing, 1965). Brian Davies, O.P., *An Introduction to the Philosophy of Religion* (New York: Oxford University Press, 1982). Etienne Gilson, *The Christian Philosophy of St. Thomas Aquinas* (New York: Random House, 1956). Pope John Paul II, *Two Lectures on St. Thomas Aquinas* (Niagara, N.Y.: Niagara University Press, 1985) contains talks the Holy Father gave on November 17, 1979 and September 13, 1980, which can also be found in *The Whole Truth About Man*, Addresses of John Paul II to University Faculties and Students, edited by James V. Schall, S.J. (Boston: Daughters of St. Paul, 1981).

For an Anglican Thomist on theology, see E. L. Mascall, *Theology and the Gospel of Christ* (London: SPCK, 1977).

3. Reviving Thomism

1974 marked the seven-hundredth anniversary of the death of Thomas Aquinas and around the world there were conferences, special issues of journals, anthologies of learned interpretations of Thomas. Both *The Thomist* and *The New Scholasticism* devoted special issues to mark the anniversary. In 1979 there were commemorations of the centenary of *Aeterni Patris*. See, for example, *One Hundred Years of Thomism*, edited by Victor B. Brezik, C.S.B. (Houston, Texas: Center for Thomistic Studies, 1981). Thomas J. A. Hartley, *Thomistic Revival and the Modernist Era* (Toronto: PIMS, 1971). Philip Gleason, *Keeping the Faith: American Catholicism Past and Present* (Notre Dame, Ind.: University of Notre Dame Press, 1987). See *Albert and Thomas: Selected Writings*, translated and edited by Simon Tugwell, O.P., with a magnificent preface by Leonard E. Boyle, O.P., in Classics of Western Spirituality (New York: Paulist Press, 1988). See James A. Weisheipl, O.P., *Friar Thomas d'Aquino* (Washington, D.C.: Catholic University Press, 1983); W. H. Principe, *Thomas Aquinas's Spirituality* (Toronto: PIMS, 1984); Vernon Bourke, *The Pocket Aquinas* (New York: Pocket Books, 1960).

The essay by the American philosopher Josiah Royce, "Pope Leo's Philosophical Movement and its Relation to Modern Thought," in *Fugitive Essays* (Cambridge, Mass.: Harvard University Press, 1920) provides an interesting look at the Thomistic revival from an outside viewpoint.

On Descartes: to read the *Meditations* is a philosophical experience of the first water, as it is to read the *Discourse on Method.* Here one sees the modern turn in all its freshness and power. See *Essays on Descartes' "Meditations",* edited by Amelie Oksenberg Rorty (Berkeley, Calif.: University of California Press, 1986). Jacques Maritain's *The Dream of Descartes* (1944, reprint, Port Washington, N.Y.: Kinnikat Press, 1969) provides a French Thomist's view of Descartes. English translations of Descartes are easily found; the writings about Descartes are seemingly as numerous as the sands of the sea.

On Aristotle: there are many excellent introductions to Aristotle. Here are a few of them: Henry B. Veatch, *Aristotle* (Bloomington, Ind.: Indiana University Press, 1974); G. E. R. Lloyd, *Aristotle: The Growth and Structure of His Thought* (New York: Cambridge University Press, 1968); D. J. Allan, *The Philosophy of Aristotle,* 2d ed. (New York: Oxford University Press, 1970); Elizabeth Anscombe and Peter Geach, *Three Philosophers* (Ithaca, N.Y.: Cornell University Press, 1961), and Jonathan Lear, *Aristotle: The Desire to Understand* (Cambridge: Cambridge University Press, 1988).

Joseph Owens, *The Doctrine of Being in the Aristotelian Metaphysics* (Toronto: PIMS, 1970) is an effort to see Aristotle in independence from such medieval commentators as St. Thomas Aquinas.

4. Two Big Pictures

David B. Burrell, *Aquinas, God, and Action* (Notre Dame, Ind.: University of Notre Dame Press, 1979); Mary Clark, introduction to her *An Aquinas Reader* (New York: Fordham University Press, 1988); A. G. Sertillanges, *St. Thomas Aquinas and His Work* (London: Burns, Oates, and Washbourne, 1932); A. Waltz, *St. Thomas Aquinas* (Westminster, Md.: Newman, 1951). See Joseph M. Boyle, Germain Grisez, and Olaf Tollefsen, *Free Choice: A Self-Referential Argument* (Notre Dame, Ind.: University of Notre Dame, 1976) for the kind of argument used in this chapter. Mark D. Jordan, *Ordering Wisdom: The Hierarchy of Philosophical Discourses in Aquinas* (Notre Dame, Ind.: University of Notre Dame Press, 1986).

On Modernity, see David Frisby, *Fragments of Modernity* (Cambridge, Mass.: MIT Press, 1986); Alasdair MacIntyre, *After Virtue,* 2d. ed.

(Notre Dame, Ind.: University of Notre Dame Press, 1981) and *Whose Justice? Which Rationality?* (Notre Dame, Ind.: University of Notre Dame Press, 1988); Jurgen Habermas, *The Philosophical Discourse of Modernity* (Cambridge, Mass.: MIT Press, 1987).

See James Collins, *Three Paths in Philosophy* (Chicago: Regnery, 1962) which contains, among other essays, "Leo XIII and the Philosophical Approach to Modernity," and "Thomism in College." Jacques Maritain's *The Peasant of the Garonne* (New York: Henry Holt, 1968) is a wise and wily look at the modern philosophical scene. See, too, George William Rutler, *Beyond Modernity* (San Francisco: Ignatius Press, 1987).

5. Thomas's Big Picture

The various surveys by Bourke, Gilson, Maritain, Pieper, Weisheipl, and myself are relevant to this discussion. See Erwin Panofsky, *Gothic Architecture and Scholasticism* (New York: New American Library Reprint, 1976). On the sorting out of philosophical labor, see *The Division and Methods of the Sciences*, a translation by Armand Maurer of portions of St. Thomas's commentary on Boethius' *De trinitate* (Toronto: PIMS, 1953). F. Van Steenberghen, *Aristotle in the West* (Louvain: Nauwelaerts, 1955) and *St. Thomas and Heterodox Aristotelianism* (Washington, D.C.: Catholic University Press, 1979). See Etienne Gilson, *Thomist Realism and the Critique of Knowledge*, translated by Mark A. Wauck (San Francisco: Ignatius Press, 1986). The great Thomists of the revival are all but unanimous on the opposition stated in the Handbook though they express it in more complicated ways. There is, however, a school of "Transcendental Thomism" which stems from Pierre Marechal and which includes Karl Rahner and Bernard Lonergan and W. Norris Clarke; this school, too simply, takes the modern critique of realism very seriously and tries to re-express Thomism in a way that does not run afoul of that critique. See Bernard Lonergan, *Insight* (New York: Philosophical Library, 1957); Karl Rahner, *Spirit in the World* (New York: Herder and Herder, 1968); and Gerald McCool, S.J., "The Tradition of Saint Thomas in North America: At 50 Years," *The Modern Schoolman* (March 1988): 185–206. See as well *The Thomist Spectrum* by Helen James John, S.N.D. (New York: Fordham University Press, 1966).

The most readable and accessible work on Thomas remains that of G. K. Chesterton, *St. Thomas Aquinas* (New York: Doubleday Anchor Books, 1956). The basic biographical documents will be found in Kenelm Foster, *The Life of Saint Thomas Aquinas* (London: Longmans, 1959). See, too, William Wallace's article, "Thomas Aquinas" in the *New Catholic Encyclopedia* (1966), vol. 14, 102–115.

6. Theologian as Philosopher

Etienne Gilson, *The Philosopher and Theology* (New York: Random House, 1961); Simon Tugwell, O.P., Introduction to Aquinas in *Albert and Thomas: Selected Writings* (New York: Paulist Press, 1988). See Weisheipl's *Friar Thomas d'Aquino*, already mentioned. For a magnificent panorama of Thomas's thought as it ascends from knowledge of the natural world through metaphysics, theology to that wisdom which is the gift of the Holy Ghost, see Jacques Maritain, *The Degrees of Knowledge* (London: Geoffrey Bles, 1959). See chapter 12 in Josef Pieper, *Guide to Thomas Aquinas* (New York: Pantheon, 1962).

During the 1930s, because of the claim by Emile Brehier that Christian Philosophy is a contradiction in terms, a great many Thomists wrote books on just that subject. Jacques Maritain, *Christian Philosophy* (New York: Philosophical Library, 1955) and Etienne Gilson, *Christianity and Philosophy* (New York: Sheed and Ward, 1939) convey the spirit of the debate. Chapter 3 of my *Thomism in an Age of Renewal* is entitled "Philosophy and Faith."

7. What Is a Thing?

The assumption of this introductory presentation is that Thomas's acceptance of Aristotle's philosophy was decisive and central to this thought. Of course, this does not mean that Thomas's philosophy was identical to Aristotle's—he took arguments and doctrines from every source available to him. But it does mean that doctrines became part of his philosophy to the degree that they were compatible with its fundamental Aristotelian base.

Twenty-five years ago, various Thomists had developed a variety of interpretations of Thomas's natural philosophy and its relation to modern science. See Maritain, *Science and Wisdom* (London: Geoffrey Bles, 1944); Charles deKoninck, *The Hollow Universe*, reprint (Ox-

ford: Oxford University Press, 1957). For some, natural philosophy
was a branch of metaphysics. Cf. Fernand van Steenberghen, *Episte-
mology* (New York: J. F. Wagner, 1944). See William A. Wallace, *Pre-
lude to Galileo*, Boston Studies in Philosophy of Science, volume 62
(Boston: D. Reidel, 1981) and *From a Realist Point of View* (New York:
University Press of America, 1983).

See Leo Elder's essay "Saint Thomas Aquinas' Commentary on the
Physics of Aristotle," and William Wallace, "St. Thomas's Conception
of Natural Philosophy and its Method," in *La Philosophie de la Nature
de Saint Thomas d'Aquin*, a publication of the Pontifical Academy of
St. Thomas, edited by Leo Elders, S.V.D., Rome, 1982.

8. Art and Nature

For Thomas, as for Aristotle, 'art' meant chiefly the imposition by
humans of some new form on natural material for one purpose or
another. Such humble activities as shoemaking come immediately to
mind. But at the same time they readily used examples of sculpture,
a fine art. Aristotle's *Poetics* is the mandatory point of reference for
any discussion of art as a making which is an imitation of human action. Thomists like Jacques Maritain, taking clues and hints from the
text of Thomas, developed what might be called a Thomistic aesthetics. See *Art and Scholasticism* (Notre Dame, Ind.: University of Notre
Dame Press, 1974) and *Creative Intuition in Art and Poetry* (Princeton,
N.J.: Princeton University Press, 1953). Francis Kovach, *The Aesthetics
of Beauty* (Norman, Okla.: Oklahoma University Press, 1976). On the
transcendental properties of being, see now Jan Aertsen, *Nature and
Creature: Thomas Aquinas's Way of Thought* (Leiden: Brill, 1988). James
Joyce, in *The Portrait of the Artist as a Young Man*, has Stephen Daeda-
lus cite Thomas's definition of beauty. Predictably, perhaps, there is
a book, *Joyce and Aquinas*, by William T. Noon, S.J. (New Haven,
Conn.: Yale University Press, 1957).

9. Causes

A paradoxical feature of modernity is that it both questions our
ability to know causes and speaks of the world as causally determined,
excluding from it chance or indeterminism. While a principle of indeterminism has been admitted in physical theory, philosophers con-

tinue to ask how free human action is compatible with a determined physical universe. See Stanley Jaki, *The Relevance of Physics* (Chicago: University of Chicago Press, 1966) and his Gifford Lectures, *The Road of Science and the Ways of God,* Edinburgh, 1975–76. *On The Threshold of Exact Science: Selected Writings of Anneliese Maier on Late Medieval Natural Philosophy,* edited by Steven D. Sargent (Philadelphia: University of Pennsylvania Press, 1982). Richard J. Blackwell, *Discovery in the Physical Sciences* (Notre Dame, Ind.: University of Notre Dame Press, 1969).

10. Parmenides' Problem

Joseph Bobik, *Aquinas on Being and Essence* (Notre Dame, Ind.: University of Notre Dame Press, 1965). Jacques Maritain, *A Preface to Metaphysics* (New York: Sheed and Ward, 1948).

11. Motion

John N. Deely and Raymond J. Nogar, *The Problem of Evolution* (New York: Appleton Century Croft, 1973). Yves Simon, *The Great Dialogue of Nature and Space* (Albany, N.Y.: Magi Books, 1970).

12. Creation

See Stanley Jaki, *Cosmos and Creator* (Chicago: Gateway Editions, 1980).

13. Soul

See Peter Geach, *God and the Soul* (New York: Schocken Books, 1969).

14. Beyond the Grave

Anton Pegis, "The Separated Soul and Its Nature in St. Thomas," in *St. Thomas Aquinas 1274–1974 Commemorative Studies* (Toronto: PIMS, 1974), volume 1, pp. 131 ff.

15. Metaphor and Analogy

Mortimer J. Adler, *Some Questions about Language* (LaSalle, Ill.: Open Court, 1976). Ralph McInerny, *The Logic of Analogy* (The Hague: Nijhoff, 1961) and *Studies in Analogy* (The Hague: Nijhoff, 1966). Owen Barfield, *Poetic Diction: A Study in Meaning* (New York: McGraw-Hill, 1964). Walker Percy, *The Message in the Bottle* (New York: Farrar, Straus and Giroux, 1975).

16. Proving God Exists

See Reginald Garrigou-Lagrange, *The One God* (London: Herder, 1943). David Burrell, C.S.C., *Exercises in Religious Understanding* (Notre Dame, Ind.: University of Notre Dame Press, 1974) for interesting discussions of Anselm and Aquinas. Henri de Lubac, S.J., *The Discovery of God* (Chicago: Regnery, 1967). Robert Sokolowski, *The God of Faith and Reason* (Notre Dame, Ind.: University of Notre Dame Press, 1982). W. Norris Clarke, S.J., *The Philosophical Approach to God: A Neo-Thomist Perspective* (Winston-Salem, N.C.: Wake Forest University Press, 1979). *Quinque Sunt Viae*, edited by Leo Elders, *Studi Tomistici* 9 (Rome: Pontifical Academy of St. Thomas Aquinas, 1980).

17. Speaking of God

Brian Davies, O.P., *Thinking About God* (London: Geoffrey Chapman, 1985). David Burrell, *Analogy and Philosophical Language* (New Haven, Conn.: Yale University Press, 1973). Battista Mondin, *The Principle of Analogy in Protestant and Catholic Theology* (The Hague: Nijhoff, 1963).

18. The Meaning of Life

John Finnis, *Fundamentals of Ethics* (New York: Fordham University Press, 1983); *Natural Law and Natural Rights* (Oxford: Clarendon Press, 1980); Russell Hittinger, *The New Natural Law Theory* (Notre Dame, Ind.: University of Notre Dame Press, 1988); Philip E. Devine,

The Ethics of Homicide (Ithaca, N.Y.: Cornell University Press, 1978). Germain Grisez and Joseph M. Boyle, *Life and Death with Liberty and Justice* (Notre Dame, Ind.: University of Notre Dame Press, 1979). Edward J. Capestany, *The Moral World* (Scranton, N.J.: Ridge Row Press, 1988). Ralph McInerny, *Ethica Thomistica* (Washington, D.C.: Catholic University Press, 1982). Stephen Theron, *Morals as Founded on Natural Law* (Frankfurt and New York: Peter Lang, 1987). Ronald Lawler, *Philosophical Analysis and Ethics* (Milwaukee, Wisc.: Bruce Publishing, 1968). Josef Pieper, *The Four Cardinal Virtues* (Notre Dame, Ind.: University of Notre Dame Press, 1966). Yves Simon, *The Tradition of the Natural Law* (New York: Fordham University Press, 1967).

19. On Being Good

St. Thomas Aquinas on Politics and Ethics, edited by Paul E. Sigmund (New York: Norton, 1988). *Aquinas: Selected Political Writings*, edited by A. P. D'Entreves (New York: Barnes and Noble, 1981). Henry B. Veatch, *Human Rights: Fact or Fancy?* (Baton Rouge, La.: LSU Press, 1985). Alan Donagan, *Human Ends and Human Actions: An Exploration of St. Thomas's Treatment*, Aquinas Lecture (Milwaukee, Wisc.: Marquette University Press, 1985). *Saint Thomas Aquinas on Law, Morality, and Politics*, edited by William P. Baumgarth and Richard J. Regan, S.J. (Indianapolis: Hackett, 1988). Yves Simon, *A General Theory of Authority* (Notre Dame, Ind.: University of Notre Dame Press, 1962).

20. Aristotle and the Beatific Vision

This primer presentation of Thomas Aquinas's general outlook has taken his relationship to Aristotle to be largely unproblematic and has stressed the importance of Thomas's commentaries on Aristotle. This is, of course, an area where all points are contested. See M. D. Chenu, *A Guide to the Study of Thomas Aquinas* (Chicago: University of Chicago Press, 1964); Henry Jaffe, *Thomism and Aristotelianism* (Chicago: University of Chicago Press, 1952). See Mark Jordan's *Ordering Wisdom*, already mentioned, and my *Boethius and Aquinas* (Washington, D.C.: Catholic University of America Press, 1989). Joseph Owens, "Aquinas as Aristotelian Commentator," and Vernon Bourke, "The Nicomachean Ethics and Thomas Aquinas" in *St. Thomas Aquinas 1274–1974 Commemorative Studies*, (Toronto: PIMS, 1974) volume 1, pp. 213–238 and pp. 239–259.

THOMISTIC CHRONOLOGY

1200	Charter of University of Paris.
1210	Prohibition against "reading" Aristotle at Paris.
1215	Founding of Order of Preachers.
	Council of Lateran.
	First statutes of University of Paris.
	Magna Carta.
1225	Birth of Saint Thomas at Roccasecca.
1230–39	Thomas at Monte Cassino.
1231	Lifting of ban on Aristotle at Paris.
1239–44	Thomas student at University of Naples.
1240	First works of Averroes become known.
1240–48	Albert the Great comments on Aristotle at Paris.
	Roger Bacon comments on Aristotle.
1244	Thomas joins Dominicans at Naples.
1244–45	Detained by family.
1245	Deposition of Frederick II.
1245–48	Thomas student at Paris.
1248	Albert the Great founds Faculty of Theology at Cologne.
1248–52	Thomas student of Albert at Cologne.
1248–54	Crusade of Saint Louis.
1248–55	St. Bonaventure teaches at Paris.
1250	Death of Frederick II.
1250/1	Thomas ordained priest.
1252–56	Bachelor of *Sentences* at Paris.
1256	Thomas Master of Theology.
1256–59	First Paris Professorate.
1259–68	Thomas in Italy.
1263	William of Moerbeke translates Aristotle for St. Thomas.
1264	Thomas writes liturgy for feast of Corpus Christi.
1266–70	Averroist controversy at Paris.
1268–72	Second Paris Professorate.

1270	First Condemnation of Averroism.
1272	Regent of Theology at Naples.
1273	Stops writing.
1274	March 7, Thomas dies at Fossanova.
1274	Council of Lyon unites East and West.
1276	*Roman de la Rose.*
1277	March 7, Condemnation at Paris of 219 Averroistic propositions, including however, some Thomistic tenets.
1323	Canonization of St. Thomas.
1325	Revocation of Paris condemnation.

THE WRITINGS OF THOMAS
IN ENGLISH TRANSLATIONS

The vast literary production of Thomas can be sorted out in a variety of ways. Weisheipl, in his catalog of the authentic works of Thomas, discusses the matter at some length and ends by adopting the classification followed in the *New Catholic Encyclopedia*. This divides the works into theological syntheses, academic disputations, expositions of Scripture, expositions of Aristotle, other expositions, polemical writings, special treatises, expert opinions, letters, liturgical works and sermons, and doubtfully authentic works.

Given the threefold task of the theologian—to dispute, comment, and preach—we might imagine classifying the works as expositions, disputations, and sermons. This would leave out a sizeable portion of the works, however, most notably the commentaries on Aristotle and various Neoplatonic writers. A feature of these works is that, while their author was a theologian, it is impossible to characterize the works as theological. The fact is that Thomas is the author of an extensive philosophical production. It is convenient, accordingly, to take the division of the writings into philosophical and theological as basic.

A. Philosophical writings

The very first work of Thomas may well be that *On Modal Propositions*, thought to have been written in 1244–45 as a letter to fellow students at Naples while Thomas was being detained by his family at Roccasecca. A work *On Fallacies* had the same addressees and was written at the same time and place. These have not been translated into English.

At Paris, before he became a Master in 1256, Thomas wrote *On Being and Essence*, masterfully rendered into English and commented on by Joseph Bobik, *Aquinas on Being and Essence* (Notre Dame, Ind.: University of Notre Dame Press, 1965).

On the Principles of Nature, English translation in Vernon Bourke, *The Pocket Aquinas* (New York: Pocket Books, 1960).

On the Rule of Princes, written in Rome about 1267, can be found in English translation by J. G. Dawson in *Aquinas: Selected Political Writings,* ed. A. P. D'Entreves, (Totowa, N.J.: Barnes & Noble, 1981). See now Paul Sigmund, editor, *St. Thomas Aquinas on Politics and Ethics,* (New York: Norton, 1988).

On Kingship, translated by G. B. Phelan and I. T. Eschmann, (Toronto: Pontifical Institute of Mediaeval Studies, 1949).

On Separate Substances, English translation as *Treatise on Separate Substances,* by F. J. Lescoe (West Hartford, Conn.: St. Joseph College, 1959).

Commentaries on Aristotle

Thomas wrote commentaries on the following works of Aristotle:

The *In Aristotelis librum peri hermeneias,* translated into English as *Aristotle: on Interpretation: Commentary by St. Thomas and Cajetan,* by Jean Oesterle (Milwaukee, Wisc.: Marquette University Press, 1962).

The *Posterior Analytics,* English translation by F. R. Larcher, *Commentary on the Posterior Analytics of Aristotle* (Albany, N.Y.: Magi Books, 1970).

The *Physics,* translated into English by R. J. Blackwell, Richard Spaeth and W. Edmund Thirkel (New Haven, Conn.: Yale University Press, 1963).

The *De coelo et mundo,* English translation as *Exposition of Aristotle's Treatise On the Heavens Books I–III,* by F. R. Larcher and P. H. Conway (Columbus, Ohio: College of St. Mary of the Springs, 1964).

On Generation and Corruption, no English translation.

On Meteors, an English translation in *Latin Treatises on the Comets,* ed. L. Thorndike (Chicago: University of Chicago Press, 1950).

The *De anima: Aristotle's De Anima with the Commentary of St. Thomas Aquinas,* translated by Foster and Humphries (New Haven, Conn.: Yale University Press, 1951).

On Sense and the Sensed Object, and *On Memory and Reminiscence,* no English translations.

Metaphysics, English translation by J. P. Rowan as *Commentary on the Metaphysics of Aristotle*, 2 volumes (Chicago: Regnery, 1964).

Nicomachean Ethics as *Commentary on the Nicomachean Ethics*, 2 volumes, translated by C. I. Litzinger (Chicago: Regnery, 1964).

Politics (incomplete). No English translation.

Other Philosophical Commentaries

Such commentaries on neoplatonic works as that on the *Book on Causes* (which Thomas correctly discerned to be excerpted from the *Elements of Theology* of Proclus) and that on Pseudo-Dionysius' *On the Divine Names* can be classified as philosophical. These are yet to be translated into English.

Thomas commented on two shorter works of Boethius.

On the *De trinitate* of Boethius, translated as *Faith, Reason and Theology* [questions 1–4], and *The Division and Methods of the Sciences* [questions 5–6] by Armand Maurer (Toronto: Pontifical Institute of Mediaeval Studies, 1987 & 1986).

On the *De hebdomadibus*, English translation by Peter O'Reilly in his doctoral dissertation, University of Toronto, 1960).

Other Philosophical Works

Such polemical works as *On the Unicity of Intellect Against the Averroists*, English translation in *The Trinity and the Unicity of the Intellect*, R. E. Brennan (St. Louis, Mo.: Herder Book Co., 1946) or as *On the Unity of the Intellect against the Averroists*, translated by Beatrice Zedler (Milwaukee, Wisc.: Marquette University Press, 1966) and *On the Eternity of the World* (Milwaukee, Wisc.: Marquette University Press, 1964) should be classified among Thomas's philosophical writings since they reveal his attitude toward the text of Aristotle. Thomas wrote as well a little work *On the Motion of the Heart* and another *On the Mixing of Elements*, yet another *On Buying and Selling on Time*. This last is translated by A. O'Rahilly as "On Buying and Selling on Credit" in *Irish Ecclesiastical Record* 31 (1928): 164–165. His works on casting lots, on consulting astrologers, and the hidden operations of nature may be mentioned here as well as the little work *How to Study* (*De modo studendi*). This last is translated into English in *Life of the Spirit*, V. White (Oxford: Blackfriars, 1944, Suppl. pp. 161–180).

B. Theological writings

Thomas's work *On the Sentences* of Peter Lombard, the compendium in four books by the twelfth-century bishop of Paris, has its origin in Thomas's work as bachelor of theology at Paris. This remains untranslated into English.

Biblical Commentaries

On *Job*, English translation by Martin Yaffe and Anthony Damico (Atlanta, Ga.: Scholars Press, 1989).

On the *Psalms* (1–54), not yet translated into English.

On *Isaiah*, not yet translated into English.

On *Jeremiah* (incomplete) still to be translated into English.

On the *Lamentations* of Jeremiah. Not yet in English.

The *Golden Chain (Catena Aurea)*. The English translation bears the Latin title, *Catena Aurea*, 4 volumes (Oxford, 1841–45). This is a continuous gloss on the four Gospels gleaned from the Latin and Greek Fathers and undertaken at the wish of Pope Urban IV.

We have commentaries on *Matthew* and *John*, though these were taken down by another, the latter by Reginald of Piperno, a fellow Dominican. There is an English translation of the commentary on John's Gospel as *Commentary on the Gospel of John* by J. A. Weisheipl and F. R. Larcher (Albany, N.Y.: Magi Books, 1980).

Thomas commented on all the *Epistles of St. Paul.*

Commentary on St. Paul's Epistle to the Galatians, translated by F. R. Larcher (Albany, N.Y.: Magi Books, 1966).

Commentary on St. Paul's Epistle to the Ephesians, translated by M. L. Lamb (Albany, N.Y.: Magi Books, 1966).

Commentary on St. Paul's First Letter to the Thessalonians and the Letter to the Philippians, translated by F. R. Larcher and Michael Duffy (Albany, N.Y.: Magi Books, 1981).

Summaries of Theology

The *Summa contra gentiles*, in four books, was written at the behest of St. Raymond Penafort, as an aid to Dominican missionaries preaching against Moslems, Jews, and Christian heretics in Spain and is dated as of 1259–64 by Weisheipl. English translation by Pegis, Anderson,

Bourke, O'Neil, originally published by Doubleday in 1955–57, now available in paperback from University of Notre Dame Press.

The great unfinished *Summa theologiae* was begun after Thomas returned to Italy, perhaps in 1266. Part One was completed in 1268. The Second Part spanned the years 1269–72, the second Parisian regency, the *prima secundae* finished about 1270 and the *secunda secundae* in 1272. The Third Part, never finished, was begun at Naples in 1272. English translation in five volumes as *Summa theologica* by the Fathers of the English Dominican Province, reprint (Westminster, Md.: Christian Classics, 1981).

Thomas also began but did not complete a *Compendium of Theology* for his companion Reginald of Piperno; the work is placed late in his life, perhaps also written at Naples. Translated into English by C. Vollert (St. Louis: B. Herder Book Co., 1948).

The *Disputed Questions* and the *Quodlibetal Questions* are fairly direct results of Thomas's magisterial activity. Scholars disagree as to the dating of the particular disputed questions but it seems safe to say that they span Thomas's magisterial career.

Disputed Questions

The former include the massive collection in 29 questions, *On Truth,* English translation in 3 volumes by Mulligan, McGlynn, Schmidt (Chicago: Regnery, 1952–54).

Disputed Question On Evil, English translation by John and Jean Oesterle, to appear shortly from University of Notre Dame Press.

On the Power of God, English translation by L. Shapcote in 3 volumes, reprint (Westminster, Md.: Newman, 1952).

The Cardinal Virtues, On the Virtues in General, On Spiritual Creatures, On Charity, and *On Fraternal Correction, On the Union of the Incarnate Word,* translated into English as *On the Virtues in General,* by J. P. Reid (Providence, R.I.: Providence College Press, 1951).

On Charity, translated by L. H. Kendzierski (Milwaukee, Marquette University Press, 1960).

On Spiritual Creatures, translated by Fitzpatrick and Wellmuth (Milwaukee, Wisc.: Marquette University Press, 1951).

On the Soul, translated by J. P. Rowan (St. Louis, Mo.: B. Herder Book Co., 1949); and as *Questions on the Soul* by James H. Robb (Milwaukee, Wisc.: Marquette University Press, 1984).

There is no English translation of the *Disputed Question on the Incarnate Word.*

Quodlibetal Questions

The 12 quodlibetal questions that have come down to us are also the subject of much discussion as to the place and date of their occurrence. There is no question as to the time of year, since this academic exercise was scheduled for Christmas and Easter. Weisheipl divided them into two groups, according to the two Parisian periods. There is an English translation of the first two as *Quodlibetal questions 1 and 2,* translated by Sandra Edwards (Toronto: Pontifical Institute of Mediaeval Studies, 1983).

Polemical Works

Some of Thomas's philosophical writings address the Latin Averroist controversy. He also wrote against the secular masters who attacked the religious vocation of the mendicants. *Against Those Impugning the Cult of God and Religion* is one of these, dating from perhaps 1256, translated into English as *An Apology for the Religious Orders* by J. Proctor, reprint (Westminster, Md.: Newman, 1950). This book also contains Thomas's work *Against those who would Prevent Boys from Entering Religion.*

On the Perfection of the Spiritual Life is available in a printed English translation as *The Religious State: The Episcopate and the Priestly Office* (Westminster, Md.: Newman Press, 1950).

On the Errors of the Greeks, meaning the Eastern church. No English translation.

He wrote a work on the faith directed against Saracens, Greeks, and Armenians at the request of the Cantor of Antioch in 1264, still untranslated into English.

For a more complete listing of the writings of St. Thomas, see James Weisheipl, O.P., *Friar Thomas d'Aquino: His Life, Thought and Work,* 2d ed. (Washington, D.C.: Catholic University of America Press, 1983).